LEAN & GREEN COOKBOOK

100+ *Fantastic Recipes* to unleash your imagination in the kitchen!

Stay ***Healthy*** and ***Fit*** with Easy and

Green Meals for ***every type of diet you are following!***

BY

Michelle Laurie Johnson

Introduction

"We are what we Eat."

For many years, we have listened to this sentence, passed on from our grandparents to us. It is simply the truth: **our body works because we give it the right fuel by eating foods.** Scientists said that to prevent pathologies such as heart disease, diabetes, or cancer, we must eat the proper amount of nutrients every day. I agree with them! We are obsessed with the moment's diet, and the media bombard us with the right diet to follow.

However, what happens if we must frequently change our diet? Some people have to change their diet due to their health needs: they discover renal pathologies, diabetes, hypertension or simply food intolerance. So, **it happens that we must re-invented our cooking method**, our daily recipes and our Meal Plan.

This is the reason why I created this book!

Regardless of the diet you are currently following, the recipes you will find in this cookbook may help you **re-find your fantasy in the kitchen**: they are all lean and healthy!

	Federal Government Recommendation	
Calories	**Men** 19-25: 2,800 26-45: 2,600 46-65: 2,400 65+: 2,200	**Women** 19-25: 2,200 26-50: 2,000 51+: 1,800
Total fat (% of Calorie Intake)	20%-35%	
Total Carbohydrates (% of Calorie Intake)	45%-65%	
Sugars	N/A	
Fiber	**Men** 19-30: 34 g. 31-50: 31 g. 51+: 28 g.	**Women** 19-30: 28 g. 31-50: 25 g. 51+: 22 g
Protein	10%-35%	
Sodium	Under 2,300 mg.	
Potassium	At least 4,700 mg.	
Calcium	**Men** 1,000 mg.	**Women** 19-50: 1,000 mg. 51+: 1,200 mg

The Lean & Green recipes are the fundamental elements for creating the right habits and suitable meals for every diet!

If your goal is to stay healthy, prevent heart disease and cancer, these recipes could help you assume the right nutrients.

According to **Federal Government Recommendation,** every recipe in "Lean & Green Cookbook" contains the right amount of nutrients. Each of these **can be part of your diet plan you are following!**

So, do you want to cook healthy recipes and stay fit without sacrificing taste?

Then… Let's Start!

Breakfast and Snack Recipes

TASTY BREAKFAST DONUTS

Preparation Time: 5 minutes

Cooking Time: 5 minutes

Servings: 4

Ingredients:

- 43 grams' cream cheese
- 2 eggs
- 2 tablespoons almond flour
- 2 tablespoons erythritol
- 1 ½ tablespoons coconut flour
- ½ teaspoon baking powder
- ½ teaspoon vanilla extract
- 5 drops Stevia (liquid form)
- 2 strips bacon, fried until crispy

Directions:

1. Rub coconut oil over donut maker and turn on.
2. Pulse all ingredients except bacon in a blender or food processor until smooth (should take around 1 minute).
3. Pour batter into donut maker, leaving 1/10 in each round for rising.
4. Leave for 3 minutes before flipping each donut. Leave for another 2 minutes or until fork comes out clean when piercing them. Take donuts out and let them cool.
5. Repeat steps 1-5 until all batter is used.
6. Crumble bacon into bits and use to top donuts.

CHEESY SPICY BACON BOWLS

Preparation Time: 10 minutes
Cooking Time: 22 minutes
Servings: 12
Ingredients:

- 6 strips Bacon, pan fried until cooked but still malleable
- 4 eggs
- 60 grams' cheddar cheese
- 40 grams' cream cheese, grated
- 2 Jalapenos, sliced and seeds removed
- 2 tablespoons coconut oil
- ¼ teaspoon onion powder
- ¼ teaspoon garlic powder
- Dash of salt and pepper

Directions:

1. Preheat oven to 375°F.
2. In a bowl, beat together eggs, cream cheese, jalapenos (minus 6 slices), coconut oil, onion powder, garlic powder, and salt and pepper. Using leftover bacon grease on a muffin tray, rubbing it into each insert. Place bacon wrapped inside the parameters of each insert.
3. Pour beaten mixture halfway up each bacon bowl.
4. Garnish each bacon bowl with cheese and leftover jalapeno slices (placing one on top of each).
5. Leave in the oven for about 22 minutes, or until egg is thoroughly cooked and cheese is bubbly.
6. Remove from oven and let cool until edible. Enjoy!

GOAT CHEESE ZUCCHINI KALE QUICHE

Preparation Time: 35 minutes
Cooking Time: 1 hour 10 minutes
Servings: 4
Ingredients:

- 4 large eggs
- 8 ounces' fresh zucchini, sliced
- 10 ounces' kale
- 3 garlic cloves (minced)
- 1 cup soymilk
- 1 ounce's goat cheese
- 1cup grated parmesan
- 1cup shredded cheddar cheese
- 2 teaspoons olive oil
- Salt and pepper, to taste

Directions:

1. Preheat oven to 350°F.
2. Heat 1 tsp of olive oil in a saucepan over medium-high heat. Sauté garlic for 1 minute until flavored.
3. Add the zucchini and cook for another 5-7 minutes until soft.
4. Beat the eggs and then add a little milk and Parmesan cheese.
5. Meanwhile, heat the remaining olive oil in another saucepan and add the cabbage. Cover and cook for 5 minutes until dry. Slightly grease a baking dish with cooking spray and spread the kale leaves across the bottom. Add the zucchini and top with goat cheese.
6. Pour the egg, milk and parmesan mixture evenly over the other ingredients. Top with cheddar cheese.
7. Bake for 50–60 minutes until golden brown. Check the center of the quiche, it should have a solid consistency.
8. Let chill for a few minutes before serving.

CREAM CHEESE EGG BREAKFAST

Servings: 4   **Preparation Time:** 5 minutes

Ingredients: **Cooking Time:** 5 minutes

- 2 eggs, beaten
- 1 tablespoon butter
- 2 tablespoons soft cream cheese with chives

Directions:

1. Melt the butter in a small skillet.
2. Add the eggs and cream cheese.
3. Stir and cook to desired doneness.

AVOCADO RED PEPPERS ROASTED SCRAMBLED EGGS

Preparation Time: 10 minutes
Cooking Time: 12 minutes
Servings: 3
Ingredients:

- 1/2 tablespoon butter
- Eggs, 2
- 1/2 roasted red pepper, about 1 1/2 ounces
- 1/2 small avocado, coarsely chopped, about 2 1/4 ounces
- Salt, to taste

Directions:

1. In a nonstick skillet, heat the butter over medium heat. Break the eggs into the pan and break the yolks with a spoon. Sprinkle with a little salt.
2. Stir and continue stirring until the eggs start to come out. Quickly add the bell peppers and avocado.
3. Cook and stir until the eggs suit your taste. Adjust the seasoning, if necessary. Serve!

MUSHROOM QUICKIE SCRAMBLE

Preparation Time: 10 minutes
Cooking Time: 10 minutes
Servings: 4
Ingredients:

- 3 small sized eggs, whisked
- 4 pcs. Bella mushrooms
- ½ cup of spinach
- ¼ cup of red bell peppers
- 2 deli ham slices
- 1 tablespoon of ghee or coconut oil
- Salt and pepper to taste

Directions:

1. Chop the ham and veggies.
2. Put half a tbsp of butter in a frying pan and heat until melted.
3. Sauté the ham and vegetables in a frying pan then set aside.
4. Get a new frying pan and heat the remaining butter.
5. Add the whisked eggs into the second pan while stirring continuously to avoid overcooking.
6. When the eggs are done, sprinkle with salt and pepper to taste.
7. Add the ham and veggies to the pan with the eggs. Mix well.
8. Remove from burner and transfer to a plate. Serve and enjoy.

COCONUT COFFEE AND GHEE

Preparation Time: 10 minutes
Cooking Time: 10 minutes
Servings: 5
Ingredients:
- ½ Tbsp. of coconut oil
- ½ Tbsp. of ghee
- 1 to 2 cups of preferred coffee (or rooibos or black tea)
- 1 Tbsp. of coconut or almond milk

Directions:
1. Place the almond (or coconut) milk, coconut oil, ghee and coffee in a blender (or milk frothier).
2. mix for around 10 seconds or until the coffee turns creamy and foamy.
3. Pour contents into a coffee cup.
4. Serve immediately and enjoy.

YUMMY VEGGIE WAFFLES

Preparation Time: 10 minutes
Cooking Time: 9 minutes
Servings: 3
Ingredients:
- 3 cups raw cauliflower, grated
- 1 cup cheddar cheese
- 1 cup mozzarella cheese
- ½ cup parmesan
- 1/3 cup chives, finely sliced
- 6 eggs
- 1 teaspoon garlic powder
- 1 teaspoon onion powder
- ½ teaspoon chili flakes
- Dash of salt and pepper

Directions:
1. Turn waffle maker on. In a bowl mix all the listed ingredients very well until incorporated. Once waffle maker is hot, distribute waffle mixture into the insert.
2. Let cook for about 9 minutes, flipping at 6 minutes.
3. Remove from waffle maker and set aside.
4. Repeat the previous steps with the rest of the batter until gone (should come out to 4 waffles).
5. Serve and enjoy!

OMEGA 3 BREAKFAST SHAKE

Preparation Time: 5 minutes
Cooking Time: 5 minutes
Servings: 2
Ingredients:

- 1 cup vanilla almond milk (unsweetened)
- 2 tablespoons blueberries
- 1 ½ tablespoons flaxseed meal
- 1 tablespoon MCT Oil
- ¾ tablespoon banana extract
- ½ tablespoon chia seeds
- 5 drops Stevia (liquid form)
- 1/8 tablespoon Xanthan gum

Directions:

1. In a blender, pulse vanilla almond milk, banana extract, Stevia, and 3 ice cubes.
2. When smooth, add blueberries and pulse.
3. Once blueberries are thoroughly incorporated, add flaxseed meal and chia seeds.
4. Let sit for 5 minutes. After 5 minutes, pulse again until all ingredients are nicely distributed. Serve and enjoy

LIME BACON THYME MUFFINS

Preparation Time: 10 minutes
Cooking Time: 20 minutes
Servings: 3
Ingredients:

- 3 cups of almond flour
- 4 medium-sized eggs
- 1 cup of bacon bits
- 2 tsp. of lemon thyme
- ½ cup of melted ghee
- 1 tsp. of baking soda
- ½ tsp. of salt, to taste

Directions:

1. Pre-heat oven to 350° F.
2. Put ghee in mixing bowl and melt. Add baking soda and almond flour. Put the eggs in. Add the lemon thyme (if preferred, other herbs or spices may be used). Drizzle with salt. Mix all ingredients well. Sprinkle with bacon bits.
3. Line the muffin pan with liners.
4. Spoon mixture into the pan, filling the pan to about ¾ full. Bake for about 20 minutes. Test by inserting a toothpick into a muffin.
5. If it comes out clean, then the muffins are done. Serve immediately.

GLUTEN -FREE PANCAKES

Preparation Time: 5 minutes
Cooking Time: 2 minutes
Servings: 2
Ingredients:

- 6 eggs
- 1 cup low-fat cream cheese
- 1 1/2 teaspoons baking powder
- 1 scoop protein powder
- 1/4; cup almond meal
- ¼ teaspoon salt
- 2 tablespoons coconut oil
- Fresh currant
- 1 peach
- Powder sugar (optional)

Directions:

1. Take a food processor and combine baking powder, almond flour and salt. Blend for 1 minutes, then add the eggs one after another and then the cream cheese. Blend until smooth.
2. Lightly grease a skillet with coconut oil and place over medium-high heat.
3. Pour the batter into the pan. Turn the pan gently to create round pancakes.
4. Cook for about 2 minutes on each side.
5. Garnish with sliced peach, currant and powder sugar and serve pancakes!

MUSHROOM AND SPINACH OMELET

Preparation Time: 20 minutes
Cooking Time: 20 minutes
Servings: 3
Ingredients:

- 2 tablespoons butter, divided
- 6-8 fresh mushrooms, sliced, 5 ounces
- Chives, chopped, optional
- Salt and pepper, to taste
- 1 handful baby spinach, about 1/2 ounce
- Pinch garlic powder
- 4 eggs, beaten
- 1-ounce shredded Swiss cheese

Directions:

1. In a very large saucepan, sauté the mushrooms in 1 tablespoon of butter until soft. season with salt, pepper and garlic.
2. Remove the mushrooms from the pan and keep warm. Heat the remaining tablespoon of butter in the same skillet over medium heat.
3. Beat the eggs with a little salt and pepper and add to the hot butter. Turn the pan over to coat the entire bottom of the pan with egg. Once the egg is almost out, place the cheese over the middle of the tortilla.
4. Fill the cheese with spinach leaves and hot mushrooms. Let cook for about a minute for the spinach to start to wilt. Fold the empty side of the tortilla carefully over the filling and slide it onto a plate and sprinkle with chives, if desired.
5. Alternatively, you can make two tortillas using half the mushroom, spinach, and cheese filling in each.

PROTEIN OATCAKES

Preparation Time: 10 minutes
Cooking Time: 5 minutes
Servings: 1
Ingredients:

- 70g oatmeal
- 15g protein
- 1 egg white
- ½ cup water
- ½ teaspoon cinnamon
- 60g curd
- 1 teaspoon cacao powder
- 15g sugar

Directions:

1. Mix the oatmeal, protein, egg white, and water in a bowl.
2. Preheat a saucepan to medium heat.
3. Place the mixture into the saucepan.
4. While waiting, prepare the topping by mixing the curd, cinnamon, and sugar in a second bowl.
5. Remove the oatcake from the saucepan when it becomes golden-brown.
6. Add the topping and cocoa powder.
7. Serve on a plate.

ORANGE RICOTTA PANCAKES

Preparation Time: 10 minutes
Cooking Time: 5 minutes
Servings: 1
Ingredients:

- ¾ cup all-purpose flour
- ½ tablespoon baking powder
- 2 teaspoons sugar
- ½ teaspoon salt
- 3 separated eggs
- 1 cup fresh ricotta
- ¾ cup whole milk
- ½ teaspoon pure vanilla extract
- 1 large ripe orange

Directions:
1. Mix the flour, baking powder, sugar in a large bowl. Add a pinch of salt.
2. In a separate bowl, whisk egg yolk, ricotta, milk, orange zest, and orange juice.
3. Add some vanilla extract for additional flavor. Followed by the dry ingredients to the ricotta mixture and mix adequately. Stir the egg white in a different bowl, and then gently fold it in the ricotta mixture.
4. Preheat saucepan to medium heat and brush with some butter until evenly spread.
5. Use a measuring cup to drop the batter onto the saucepan, ensure the pan is not crowded.
6. Allow cooking for 2 minutes. Flip the food when you notice the edges begin to set, and bubbles form in the center. Cook the meat for another 1 to 2 minutes. Serve with any toppings of your choice.

ASIAN SCRAMBLED EGG

Preparation Time: 10 minutes
Cooking Time: 10 minutes
Servings: 1
Ingredients:

- 1 large egg
- 1/2 teaspoons light soy sauce
- 1/8 teaspoon white pepper
- 1 tablespoon vegetable oil

Directions:
1. Beat the eggs in a bowl. Add soy sauce, one-teaspoon vegetable oil, and pepper.
2. Heat olive oil in a saucepan on medium. Then add the mixture of the beaten egg.
3. The edges will begin to cook. Lessen the heat to medium and carefully scramble the eggs.
4. Turn off heat and transfer into a bowl. Serve hot and enjoy!

ARTICHOKE FRITTATAS

Preparation Time: 10 minutes
Cooking Time: 30 minutes
Servings: 1
Ingredients:

- 2.5 oz. dry spinach
- 1/4 red bell pepper
- Artichoke (drain the liquid)
- Green onions
- Dried tomatoes
- Two eggs
- Italian seasoning

- Salt
- Pepper

Directions:

1. Preheat oven to medium heat. Brush a bit of oil on the cast-iron skillet.
2. Mix all the vegetables and add some seasoning.
3. Spread the vegetables evenly in the pan.
4. Whisk the eggs and add some milk. Add some salt and pepper.
5. Mix in some cheese (helps to make it fluffier).
6. Pour the egg mixture in the saucepan. Place the pan inside the oven for about 30 minutes. Enjoy!

CHOCOLATE SWEET POTATO PUDDING

Preparation Time: 5 minutes

Cooking Time: 2 minutes

Servings: 1

Ingredients:

- 2 well-cooked sweet potatoes
- 2 tablespoons cocoa powder
- 2 tablespoons maple syrup
- ¼ cups plant-based milk (for ex. almond milk)
- ¼ tablespoons salt
- ¼ tablespoons vanilla extract

Directions:

1. Inside the food processor, put all the ingredients.
2. Blend thoroughly for about 30 seconds to 1 minute. Voilà!

PEANUT BUTTER AND PROTEIN PANCAKE

Preparation Time: 10 minutes

Cooking Time: 15 minutes

Servings: 1

Ingredients:

- ½ cup oat flour
- ½ cup gluten-free chocolate pancake mix
- ½ cup almond milk
- 1 egg
- 1 tablespoon coconut water
- 1 tablespoon peanut butter
- Fresh fruits slices

Directions:

1. Preheat a saucepan to medium heat.
2. Mix the flour and the pancake mix in a mixing bowl. Mix the almond milk and eggs with coconut water in another bowl. Mix the dry and wet ingredients thoroughly to form a delicate batter.
3. Spray the preheated saucepan with some coconut oil.
4. Put the batter into the saucepan with a measuring cup and allow it to cook for a few minutes.
5. Allow to cool and top with peanut butter and fresh fruit slices.

ZUCCHINI FRITTATA

Preparation Time: 20 minutes

Cooking Time: 20 minutes

Servings: 1

Ingredients:

- 2 large zucchinis
- 1½ teaspoon of salt

- 2 eggs
- ½ cup chopped green onions
- 1 cup flour
- ½ teaspoon of black pepper
- 1 teaspoon of baking powder
- 2 tablespoons of oil

Directions:

1. Wash the two zucchinis.
2. Cut off the zucchinis on its ends and grate them in a large mixing bowl.
3. Stir in 1 teaspoon of salt and set aside for about 10 minutes (The salt helps to draw out the water from the zucchinis). Squeeze dry the grated zucchinis to remove as much water as possible.
4. Then followed by the two whole eggs and the chopped green onions.
5. In a bowl, mix a cup flour, ½ teaspoon of salt, ½ teaspoon of black pepper, and one teaspoon of baking powder.
6. Next, pour the contents of the smaller bowl to those of the larger bowl containing the grated zucchinis.
7. Stir them all together and make sure they are well mixed.
8. Preheat a saucepan to medium temperature and add two tablespoons of oil.
9. Add the zucchini mixture a heaping tablespoonful at a time. Sauté the mixture for about 4 minutes on each side, to achieve a golden-brown color. Add more oil to the pan if needed. Serve and enjoy!

TEX-MEX TOFU BREAKFAST TACOS

Preparation Time: 10 minutes
Cooking Time: 15 minutes
Servings: 1
Ingredients:

- 8 oz. firm tofu
- 1 cup well-cooked black bean
- 1/4 red onion
- 1 cup fresh coriander
- 1 ripe avocado
- 1/2 cup salsa
- 1 medium-sized lime
- 5 whole corn tortillas
- 1/2 teaspoon garlic powder
- 1/2 teaspoon chili powder
- 1/8 teaspoon of sea salt
- 1 tablespoon salsa
- 1 tablespoon water

Directions:

1. Dice the red onions, avocados, coriander, and keep in separate bowls.
2. Also, slice the limes and keep in individual bowls. Wrap the tofu and place under a cast-iron skillet.
3. In the meantime, heat a saucepan to medium heat and cook the black beans, add a little amount of salt, cumin, and chili powder. Then decrease the heat to a low simmer and set aside.
4. Add the tofu spices and salsa into a bowl, then add some water and set aside.
5. Heat another skillet to medium heat. Pour some oil into the skillet, and then crumble the tofu into it.
6. Stir-fry for about 5 minutes until the tofu begins to brown. Add some seasoning and continue to cook for about 5 to 10 minutes, and then set aside. Heat the tortillas in oven to 250°F.
7. Top the tortillas with tofu scramble, avocado, salsa, coriander, black beans, and lime juice. Serve immediately.

MOCHA OATMEAL

Preparation Time: 5 minutes
Cooking Time: 10 minutes
Servings: 1
Ingredients:

- 1 banana
- ½ cup oats
- 1 cup coffee
- ¼ teaspoon salt
- 1 teaspoon walnut
- ½ teaspoon cacao powder
- 1 cup milk
- Honey

Directions:

1. Preheat a saucepan to medium heat. Put the oats in a saucepan.
2. Slice the banana, mash them, and add them to the oats. Add coffee, walnuts, cacao powder, and salt.
3. Stir and you may want to wait for it to simmer, practically until the mixture becomes sticky inconsistency.
4. Serve in a bowl and add milk and honey as desired. Enjoy!

BLACK AND BLUEBERRY PROTEIN SMOOTHIE

Preparation Time: 5 minutes

Cooking Time: 0 minutes

Servings: 1

Ingredients:

- 1 cup sugar-free coconut milk (or any other plant-based milk of your choice)
- 1 scoop vanilla or natural protein powder
- 6 oz. fat-free vanilla Greek yogurt
- 2 tablespoons of milled flaxseed
- 1 cup berries (black or blue)
- 1 cup ice

Directions:
1. In the food processor, place all the ingredients.
2. Blend until smooth.
3. Pour into a cup and enjoy.

SHAKE CAKE FUELING

Preparation Time: 5 minutes

Cooking Time: 0 minutes

Servings: 1

Ingredients:

- 1 packet protein shakes.
- ¼ teaspoon baking powder
- 2 tablespoons eggbeaters or egg whites
- 2 tablespoons water.

Directions:
1. Begin by preheating the oven.
2. Mix all the ingredients begin with the dry ingredients first before adding the wet ingredients.
3. After the mixture/batter is ready, pour gently into muffin cups.
4. Inside the oven, place, and bake for about 16–18minutes or until it is baked and ready. Allow it to cool completely. Add additional toppings of your choice and ensure your delicious shake cake is refreshing.

LEAN AND GREEN SMOOTHIE 1

Preparation Time: 5 minutes

Cooking Time: 0 minutes

Servings: 1

Ingredients:

- 2 ½ cups of kale leaves
- ¾ cup chilled apple juice
- 1 cup cubed pineapple
- ½ cup frozen green grapes
- ½ cup chopped apple

Directions:
1. Place the pineapple, apple juice, apple, frozen seedless grapes, and kale leaves in a blender.
2. Cover and blend until it's smooth.

3. Smoothie is ready and can be garnished with halved grapes if you wish.

LEAN AND GREEN SMOOTHIE 2

Preparation Time: 5 minutes

Cooking Time: 0 minutes

Servings: 1

Ingredients:

- 6 kale leaves

- 2 peeled oranges
- 2 cups mango kombucha
- 2 cups chopped pineapple
- 2 cups water

Directions:

1. Break up the oranges, place in the blender.
2. Add the mango kombucha, chopped pineapple, and kale leaves into the blender.
3. Blend everything until it is smooth. Smoothie is ready to be taken.

TROPICAL GREENS SMOOTHIE

Preparation Time: 5 Minutes

Cooking Time: 0 Minutes

Servings: 1

Ingredients:

- 1/2 large navel orange, peeled and segmented
- 1 banana
- 1/2 cup frozen mango chunks

- 1 cup frozen spinach
- 1 celery stalk, broken into pieces
- 1 tablespoon cashew butter or almond butter
- 1/2 tablespoon spiraling
- 1/2 tablespoon ground flaxseed
- 1/2 cup unsweetened nondairy milk
- Water, for thinning (optional)

Directions:

1. In a high-speed blender or food processor, combine the bananas, orange, mango, spinach, celery, cashew butter, spiraling (if using), flaxseed, and milk.
2. Blend until creamy, adding more milk or water to thin the smoothie if too thick. Serve immediately!

VITAMIN C SMOOTHIE CUBES

Preparation Time: 5 minutes

Cooking Time: 8 hours to chill

Servings: 1

Ingredients:

- 1/8 large papaya
- 1/8 mango

- 1/4 cups chopped pineapple, fresh or frozen
- 1/8 cup raw cauliflower florets, fresh or frozen
- 1/4 large navel oranges, peeled and halved
- 1/4 large orange bell pepper stemmed, seeded, and coarsely chopped

Directions:

1. Halve the papaya and mango, remove the pits, and scoop their soft flesh into a high-speed blender.
2. Add the pineapple, cauliflower, oranges, and bell pepper. Blend until smooth.
3. Evenly divide the puree between 2 (16-compartment) ice cube trays and place them on a level surface in your freezer. Freeze for at least 8 hours.
4. The cubes can be left in the ice cube trays until use or transferred to a freezer bag. The frozen cubes are good for about three weeks in a standard freezer or up to 6 months in a chest freezer.

OVERNIGHT CHOCOLATE CHIA PUDDING

Preparation Time: 2 minutes

Cooking Time: Overnight to Chill

Servings: 1

Ingredients:

- 1/8 cup chia seeds
- 1/2 cup unsweetened nondairy milk
- 1 tablespoon raw cacao powder
- 1/2 teaspoon vanilla extract
- 1/2 teaspoon pure maple syrup

Directions:

1. Stir together the chia seeds, milk, cacao powder, vanilla, and maple syrup in a large bowl. Divide between 2 (½-pint) covered glass jars or containers. Refrigerate overnight. Stir before serving.

SLOW COOKER SAVORY BUTTERNUT SQUASH OATMEAL

Preparation Time: 15 minutes
Cooking Time: 6 to 8 hours
Servings: 1
Ingredients:

- 1/4 cup steel-cut oats
- 1/2 cups cubed (½-inch pieces) peeled butternut squash
- 3/4 cups water
- 1/16 cup unsweetened nondairy milk
- 1/4 tablespoon chia seed
- 1/2 teaspoons yellow (mellow) miso paste
- 3/4 teaspoons ground ginger
- 1/4 tablespoon sesame seed, toasted
- 1/4 tablespoon chopped scallion, green parts only
- Shredded carrot, for serving (optional)

Directions:

1. In a slow cooker, combine the oats, butternut squash, and water. Cover the slow cooker and cook on low for 6 to 8 hours, or until the squash is fork-tender. Using a potato masher or heavy spoon, roughly mash the cooked butternut squash. Stir to combine with the oats.
2. Whisk together the milk, chia seeds, miso paste, and ginger to combine in a large bowl. Stir the mixture into the oats. Top your oatmeal bowl with sesame seeds and scallion for more plant-based fiber, top with shredded carrot.

CARROT CAKE OATMEAL

Preparation Time: 10 minutes
Cooking Time: 15 minutes
Servings: 1
Ingredients:

- 1/8 cup pecans
- 1/2 cup finely shredded carrot
- 1/4 cup old-fashioned oats
- 5/8 cups unsweetened nondairy milk
- 1/2 tablespoon pure maple syrup
- 1/2 teaspoon ground cinnamon
- 1/2 teaspoon ground ginger
- 1/8 teaspoon ground nutmeg
- 1 tablespoon chia seed

Directions:

1. Over medium-high heat in a skillet, toast the pecans for 3 to 4 minutes, often stirring, until browned and fragrant (watch closely, as they can burn quickly). Pour the pecans onto a cutting board and coarsely chop them. Set aside.
2. In an 8-quart pot over medium-high heat, combine the carrot, oats, milk, maple syrup, cinnamon, ginger, and nutmeg. When it is already boiling, reduce the heat to medium-low. Cook, uncovered, for 10 minutes, stirring occasionally. Stir in the chopped pecans and chia seeds. Serve immediately.

SPICED SORGHUM AND BERRIES

Preparation Time: 5 minutes
Cooking Time: 1 hour
Servings: 1
Ingredients:

- 1/4 cup whole-grain sorghum
- 1/4 teaspoon ground cinnamon
- 1/4 teaspoon Chinese five-spice powder
- 3/4 cups water
- 1/4 cup unsweetened nondairy milk

- 1/4 teaspoon vanilla extract
- 1/2 tablespoons pure maple syrup
- 1/2 tablespoon chia seed
- 1/8 cup sliced almonds
- 2 cups fresh raspberries, divided

Directions:

1. Using a large pot over medium-high heat, stir together the sorghum, cinnamon, five-spice powder, and water. Wait for the water to a boil, cover the bank, and reduce the heat to medium-low. Cook for 1 hour, or until the sorghum is soft and chewy. If the sorghum grains are still hard, add another cup of water and cook for 15 minutes more. Using a glass measuring cup, whisk together the milk, vanilla, and maple syrup to blend. Add the mixture to the sorghum and the chia seeds, almonds, and 1 cup of raspberries. Gently stir to combine.
2. When serving, top with the remaining 1 cup of fresh raspberries.

RAW-CINNAMON-APPLE NUT BOWL

Preparation Time: 15 minutes
Cooking Time: 1 hour to chill
Servings: 1
Ingredients:

- 1 green apple halved, seeded, and cored
- 3/4 honey crisp apples, halved, seeded, and cored
- 1/4 teaspoon freshly squeezed lemon juice
- 1 pitted Medrol dates
- 1/8 teaspoon ground cinnamon
- Pinch ground nutmeg
- 1/2 tablespoons chia seeds, plus more for serving (optional)
- 1/4 tablespoon hemp seed
- 1/8 cup chopped walnuts
- Nut butter, for serving (optional)

Directions:

1. Finely dice half the green apple and honey crisp apple. With the lemon juice, store it in an airtight container while you work on the next steps. Coarsely chop the remaining apples and the dates. Transfer to a food processor and add the cinnamon and nutmeg. Check it several times if it combines, then processes for 2 to 3 minutes to puree. Stir the puree into the reserved diced apples. Stir in the chia seeds (if using), hemp seeds, and walnuts. Chill for at least 1 hour. Enjoy! Serve as is or top with additional chia seeds and nut butter (if using).

PEANUT BUTTER AND CACAO BREAKFAST QUINOA

Preparation Time: 5 minutes
Cooking Time: 10 minutes
Servings: 1
Ingredients:

- 1/3 cup quinoa flakes
- 1/2 cup unsweetened nondairy milk
- 1/2 cup water
- 1/8 cup raw cacao powder
- 1 tablespoon natural creamy peanut butter
- 1/8 teaspoon ground cinnamon
- 1 banana, mashed
- Fresh berries of choice, for serving
- Chopped nuts of choice, for serving

Directions:

1. Using an 8-quart pot over medium-high heat, stir together the quinoa flakes, milk, water, cacao powder, peanut butter, and cinnamon. Cook and stir it until the mixture begins to simmer. Turn the heat to medium-low and cook for 3 to 5 minutes, stirring frequently.
2. Stir in the bananas and cook until hot. Serve topped with fresh berries, nuts, and a splash of milk.

VANILLA BUCKWHEAT PORRIDGE

Preparation Time: 5 minutes
Cooking Time: 25 minutes

Servings: 1
Ingredients:

- 1 cup water
- 1/4 cup raw buckwheat grouts
- 1/4 teaspoon ground cinnamon
- 1/4 banana, sliced
- 1/16 cup golden raisins
- 1/16 cup dried currants
- 1/16 cup sunflower seeds
- 1/2 tablespoons chia seeds
- 1/4 tablespoon hemp seed
- 1/4 tablespoon sesame seed, toasted
- 1/8 cup unsweetened nondairy milk
- 1/4 tablespoon pure maple syrup
- 1/4 teaspoon vanilla extract

Directions:

1. Boil the water in a pot. Stir in the buckwheat, cinnamon, and banana. Cook the mixture. Mixing it and wait for it to boil, then reduce the heat to medium-low. Cover the pot and cook for 15 minutes, or until the buckwheat is tender. Remove from the heat. Stir in the raisins, currants, sunflower seeds, chia seeds, hemp seeds, sesame seeds, milk, maple syrup, and vanilla. Cover the pot. Wait for 10 minutes before serving. Serve as is or top as desired.

BEST WHOLE WHEAT PANCAKES

Preparation Time: 10 minutes
Cooking Time: 20 minutes
Servings: 1
Ingredients:

- 3/4 tablespoons ground flaxseed
- 2 tablespoons warm water
- 1/2 cups whole wheat pastry flour
- 1/8 cup rye flour
- 1/2 tablespoons double-acting baking powder
- 1/4 teaspoon ground cinnamon
- 1/8 teaspoon ground ginger
- 1 cup unsweetened nondairy milk
- 3/4 tablespoons pure maple syrup
- 1/4 teaspoon vanilla extract

Directions:

Mix the warm water and flaxseed in a large bowl. Set aside for at least 5 minutes. Whisk together the pastry and rye flours, baking powder, cinnamon, and ginger to combine. Whisk together the milk, maple syrup, and vanilla in a large bowl. Make use of a spatula, fold the wet ingredients into the dry ingredients. Fold in the soaked flaxseed until fully incorporated. Heat a large skillet or nonstick griddle over medium-high heat. Working in batches, 3 to 4 pancakes at a time, add ¼-cup portions of batter to the hot skillet. Until golden brown, cook for 3 to 4 minutes each side or no liquid batter is visible.

SPICED PUMPKIN MUFFINS

Servings: 1   **Cooking Time:** 20 minutes
Ingredients: **Preparation Time:** 15 minutes

- 1/6 tablespoons ground flaxseed
- 1/24 cup water
- 1/8 cups whole wheat flour
- 1/6 teaspoons baking powder
- 5/6 teaspoons ground cinnamon
- 1/12 teaspoon baking soda
- 1/12 teaspoon ground ginger
- 1/16 teaspoon ground nutmeg
- 1/32 teaspoon ground cloves
- 1/6 cup pumpkin puree
- 1/12 cup pure maple syrup
- 1/24 cup unsweetened applesauce
- 1/24 cup unsweetened nondairy milk
- 1/2 teaspoons vanilla extract

Directions:

1. Preheat the oven to 350°F. Line a 12-cup metal muffin pan with parchment paper liners or use a silicone muffin pan.
2. First, mix the flaxseed and water in a large bowl then keep it aside. In a medium bowl, stir together the flour, baking powder, cinnamon, baking soda, ginger, nutmeg, and cloves.
3. In a medium bowl, stir up the maple syrup, pumpkin puree, applesauce, milk, and vanilla. Crease the wet ingredients into the dry ingredients make use of a spatula. Fold the soaked flaxseed into the batter until evenly combined, but do not over mix the batter, or your muffins will become dense. Spoon about ¼ cup of batter per muffin into your prepared muffin pan. Bake for 18 to 20 minutes, or until a toothpick inserted into the center of a muffin comes out clean. Remove the muffins from the pan. Transfer to a wire rack for cooling. Store in an airtight container that is at room temperature.

ORANGE RESOLUTION SMOOTHIE

Preparation Time: 5 minutes
Cooking Time: 0 minutes
Servings: 1
Ingredients:

- 1/4 cup orange juice
- 1/2 cup Greek yogurt
- 1/2 cup frozen mango chunks
- 1 banana, peeled, frozen
- 1/4 cup miniature carrots
- 1/2 cup frozen peach slices
- 1 tablespoon honey
- 1/4 cup pineapple pieces

Directions:

1. Gather all the ingredients.
2. Start a high-powered blender, and then add together every ingredient into it in the order mentioned in the list.
3. Turn it on for 45 to 60 seconds or more reliant on the blender, until well blended and smooth, and then divide the smoothie between two glasses. Serve straight away.

SPICY CARROT, AVOCADO, AND TOMATO SMOOTHIE

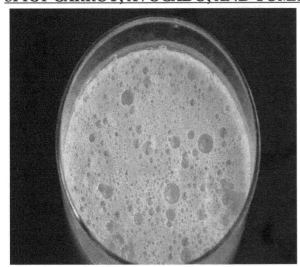

Preparation Time: 5 minutes
Cooking Time: 0 minutes
Servings: 1
Ingredients:

- 3/4 cup coconut water, unsweetened
- ½ a medium cucumber, unpeeled, chopped
- 1 medium tomato, deseeded, chopped
- 1 avocado, peeled, pitted
- 1 cup chopped romaine lettuce
- 1 medium carrot, peeled, diced
- 1 lime, peeled, halved
- 1 clove garlic, peeled
- 3/4 teaspoon sea salt
- 1/8 teaspoon cayenne pepper
- 1 tablespoon olive oil
- 1 cup ice cubes

Directions:

1. Gather all the ingredients. Add all the ingredients into it in the order cited in a blender.
2. Pulse for 45 to 60 seconds or more varying on the blender, up until well combined and smooth, and then distribute the smoothie amongst two glasses. Serve straight away.

ZUCCHINI BREAD SMOOTHIE

Preparation Time: 5 minutes
Cooking Time: 0 minutes
Servings: 1
Ingredients:

- 2 cups almond milk, unsweetened
- ½ cup baby spinach leaves, fresh, rinsed
- ½ cup rolled oats
- 2 cups chopped zucchini, fresh or frozen
- 1 teaspoon ground cinnamon
- 1 tablespoon maple syrup
- ¼ teaspoon ground nutmeg
- ¼ cup walnut halves
- 1 cup ice cubes

Directions:

1. Gather all the ingredients.
2. In a high-powered blender, add up all the ingredients into it in the sort cited in the list.
3. Turn it on for 45 to 60 seconds or further dependent on the blender, until well mixed and smooth, and then distribute the smoothie between two glasses.
4. Serve straight away.

CAULIFLOWER AND BLUEBERRY SMOOTHIE

Preparation Time: 5 minutes
Cooking Time: 0 minutes
Servings: 1
Ingredients:

- 1 cup Greek yogurt, unsweetened
- 2 tablespoons peanut butter
- 1 ¼ cup cauliflower florets, frozen
- 1 clementines, peeled
- ½ cup spinach leaves, rinsed
- 1 cup blueberries, frozen

Directions:

1. Gather all the ingredients.
2. Socket a high-powdered blender, and later combine all the components into it in the order mentioned in the ingredients list. Let it blend for 45 to 60 seconds or more reliant on the blender, until properly mixed and smooth. Then, divide the smoothie between two glasses. Serve straight away.

BUTTERNUT SQUASH SMOOTHIE

Preparation Time: 5 minutes
Cooking Time: 0 minutes
Servings: 1
Ingredients:

- 2 cups almond milk, unsweetened
- ½ cup water
- 1 cup butternut squash pieces, frozen
- 2 bananas, peeled, frozen
- 1 cup raspberries, frozen
- 2 tablespoons hemp seeds
- 1 tablespoons chia seeds
- 1 teaspoon ground cinnamon
- 1/4 cup peanut butter

Directions:

1. In a high-powdered blender, add all the ingredients into it in the order in the list.
2. Turn it on for 45 to 60 seconds or further differing on the blender, until perfectly combined and smooth, and then distribute the smoothie among two glasses. Serve up straight away.

AVOCADO AND KALE SUPER FOOD SMOOTHIE

Preparation Time: 5 minutes
Cooking Time: 0 minutes
Servings: 1
Ingredients:

- 1/2 cup almond milk, unsweetened
- 1/2 cup blueberry yogurt
- 1 banana, peeled, frozen
- 1/2 avocado, peeled, pitted
- 1 cup kale, stemmed, rinsed

Directions:
1. Gather all the ingredients.
2. Plug in a high-powered blender, and then add every one of the ingredients listed.
3. Turn it on for 45 to 60 seconds or extra dependent on the blender, until properly combined and smooth, and then divide the smoothie between two glasses. Serve straight away.

PINEAPPLE CELERY SMOOTHIE
Preparation Time: 5 minutes
Cooking Time: 0 minutes
Servings: 1
Ingredients:
- 1/4 cup almond milk, unsweetened
- 1/2 pear, cored, chopped
- 1 stalk celery, chopped
- 1/2 banana, peeled, frozen
- 1/2 teaspoon honey
- 1/2 cup pineapple pieces, cubed

Directions:
1. Gather all the ingredients.
2. Plug in a high-powdered blender, and then add all the ingredients into it in the order mentioned in the list.
3. Turn it on for 45 to 60 seconds or more depending on the blender, until well blended and smooth, and then distribute the smoothie between two glasses. Serve straight away.

MANGO AND CUCUMBER SMOOTHIE

Preparation Time: 5 minutes
Cooking Time: 0 minutes
Servings: 1
Ingredients:
- 1 ½ cup coconut milk, unsweetened
- 4 teaspoons lime juice
- 1 cup baby spinach leaves, fresh, rinsed
- 2 cup mango pieces, fresh or frozen
- 4 mint leaves, rinsed
- 1 cup chopped cucumber, deseeded, peeled
- 1/4 teaspoon cayenne pepper
- 1 cup ice cubes

Directions:
1. Collect all the ingredients.
2. Plug in a high-powered blender and all the ingredients into it in the directive mentioned in the list.
3. Pulse for 45 to 60 seconds or extra depending on the blender, up until well combined and smooth, and then distribute the smoothie between two glasses. Serve straight away.

MELON, KALE, AND BROCCOLI SMOOTHIE
Preparation Time: 5 minutes
Cooking Time: 0 minutes
Servings: 1
Ingredients:

- 2 cups coconut water, unsweetened
- 2/3 cup broccoli florets
- 2 cups honeydew melon pieces
- 1 lime, peeled, deseeded, halved
- ½ cup kale, stemmed, rinsed
- 2 Medrol dates pitted
- ½ cup mint leaves
- 1 cup ice cubes

Directions:
1. Gather all the ingredients.
2. Plug in a high-powered blender, and then add all the ingredients in the order indicated in the list.
3. Pulse for 45 to 60 seconds or extra diverging on the blender, until well mixed and smooth out, and then distribute the smoothie between two glasses. Serve straight away.

AVOCADO AND CUCUMBER SMOOTHIE

Preparation Time: 5 minutes
Cooking Time: 0 minutes
Servings: 1
Ingredients:

- 1 cup water, chilled
- 1 large cucumber, deseeded
- 1 avocado, cored, peeled

Directions:
1. Gather all the ingredients.
2. Plug in a high-powered blender, then combine all the ingredients into it in the order mentioned in the register.
3. Thump for 45 to 60 seconds or more dependent on the blender, until nicely combined and smooth, and then divide the smoothie between two glasses. Serve straight away.

APPLE, BANANA, AND COLLARD GREENS SMOOTHIE

Preparation Time: 5 minutes
Cooking Time: 0 minutes
Servings: 1
Ingredients:

- 1 cup water, chilled
- 2 green apples, cored
- 1 large banana, peeled, frozen
- 1 ½ cup collard greens, frozen

Directions:
1. Gather all the ingredients.
2. Plug in a high-powdered blender, and then combine the whole ingredients into it in the directive mentioned in the list. Pulse for 45 to 60 seconds or more varying on the blender, until well blended and smooth, and then allocate the smoothie between two glasses. Serve straight away.

BROCCOLI AND ORANGE SMOOTHIE

Preparation Time: 5 minutes
Servings: 1
Ingredients:

- 1 cup water, chilled
- 2 broccoli heads
- 1 orange, peeled

Directions:
1. Gather all the ingredients.
2. Plug in a high-powered blender, and later add every ingredient into it in the order stated in the list.

3. Pulse for 45 to 60 seconds or more depending on the blender, until well combined and smooth, then distributing the smoothie between two glasses. Serve straight away.

SWEET KIWI AND MINT SMOOTHIE

Preparation Time: 5 minutes
Cooking Time: 0 minutes
Servings: 1
Ingredients:

- 1 cup water, chilled
- 2 kiwis, peeled
- 1 medium lemon, peeled
- ¼ cup mint leaves
- ¼ cup parsley leaves
- 2 teaspoons honey

Directions:

1. Gather all the ingredients.
2. Plug in a high-powered blender, and subsequently add all the ingredients into it in the order mentioned in the list.
3. Pulse for 45 to 60 seconds or extra differing on the blender, until perfectly combined and smooth out, and then divide the smoothie between two glasses. Serve straight away.

CUCUMBER, CELERY, AND APPLE SMOOTHIE

Preparation Time: 5 minutes
Cooking Time: 0 minutes
Servings: 1
Ingredients:

- 1/2 cup water, chilled
- 1/4 lemon, juiced
- 1/2 large stalk of celery
- 1 medium green apple, cored
- 1/2 large cucumber

Directions:

1. Gather all the ingredients.
2. Plug in a high-powdered blender, and then add all the ingredients into it in the order indicated in the list.
3. Turn it on for 45 to 60 seconds or more differing on the blender, until properly combined and smooth, and then distribute the smoothie between two glasses. Serve straight away.

Tea with Coconut

Preparation Time: 10 minutes
Cooking Time: 0 minutes;
Servings: 2
Ingredients:

- 2 tea bags, cinnamon-flavored
- 2 tbsp MCT oil
- ¼ cup coconut milk, unsweetened
- 2 cups boiling water

Directions:

1. Pour boiling water between two mugs, add a tea into each mug and let them steep for 5 minutes.
2. Meanwhile, take a small saucepan, place it over medium heat, pour in milk and heat for 3 minutes or more until hot.
3. After 5 minutes, remove tea bags from mugs, stir in milk, and MCT oil by using a milk frother until combined and then serve.

Special Lunch Recipes

Bacon Spaghetti Squash Carbonara

Preparation Time: 20 minutes

Cooking Time: 40 minutes

Servings: 4

Ingredients:

- 1 small spaghetti squash
- 6 ounces' bacon (roughly chopped)
- 1 large tomato (sliced)

- 2 chives (chopped)
- 1 garlic clove (minced)
- 6 ounces' low-fat cottage cheese
- 1 cup Gouda cheese (grated)
- 2 tablespoons olive oil
- Salt and pepper, to taste

Directions:

1. Preheat the oven to 350°F.
2. Cut the squash spaghetti in half, brush with some olive oil and bake for 20–30 minutes, skin side up. Remove from the oven and remove the core with a fork, creating the spaghetti.
3. Heat one tablespoon of olive oil in a skillet. Cook the bacon for about 1 minute until crispy.
4. Quickly wipe out the pan with paper towels.
5. Heat another tablespoon of oil and sauté the garlic, tomato and chives for 2–3 minutes. Add the spaghetti and sauté for another 5 minutes, stirring occasionally to keep from burning. Begin to add the cottage cheese, about 2 tablespoons at a time. If the sauce becomes thicken, add about a cup of water. The sauce should be creamy, but not too runny or thick. Allow to cook for another 3 minutes. Serve immediately.

Cauliflower Crust Pizza

Preparation Time: 15 minutes

Cooking Time: 30–35 minutes

Servings: 1

Ingredients:

- 1/4 cauliflower (it should be cut into smaller portions)
- 1/16 grated parmesan cheese

- 1/2 egg
- ½ teaspoon Italian seasoning
- 1/16 teaspoon kosher salt
- 1 cups of freshly grated mozzarella
- 1/4 cup spicy pizza sauce.
- Basil leaves, for garnishing.

Directions:

1. Begin by preheating your oven while using the parchment paper to rim the baking sheet.
2. Process the cauliflower into a fine powder, and then transfer to a bowl before putting it into the microwave. Leave for about 5–6 minutes to get it soft.
3. Transfer the microwaved cauliflower to a clean and dry kitchen towel. Leave it to cool.
4. When cold, use the kitchen towel to wrap the cauliflower and then get rid of all the moisture by wringing the towel. Continue squeezing until water is gone completely.
5. Put the cauliflower, Italian seasoning, parmesan, egg, salt, and mozzarella (1 cup). Stir very well until well combined. Transfer the combined mixture to the baking sheet previously prepared, pressing it into a 10-inch round shape. Wait for it to bake until it becomes golden in color.
6. Take the baked crust out of the oven and use the spicy pizza sauce and mozzarella (the leftover 1 cup) to top it. Put it again inside the oven for ten more minutes until the cheese melts and looks bubbly.
7. Garnish using fresh basil leaves. You can also enjoy this with salad.

Delicious Pizza

Preparation Time: 5–10 minutes
Cooking Time: 15–20 minutes
Servings: 1
Ingredients:

- 1/4 cup mashed potato
- 1/2 egg whites
- 1/4 tablespoon baking powder
- 3/4 oz. reduced-fat shredded mozzarella
- 1/8 cup sliced white mushrooms
- 1/16 cup pizza sauce
- 3/4 oz. ground beef
- 1/4 sliced black olives
- You also need a sauté pan, baking sheets, and parchment paper

Directions:

1. Preheat the oven to 400°F.
2. Mix your baking powder and garlic potato packet. Add egg whites to your mixture and stir well until it blends.
3. Line the baking sheet with parchment paper and pour the mixed batter onto it.
4. Put another parchment paper on top of the batter and spread out the batter to a 1/8-inch circle.
5. Then place another baking sheet on top; this way, the matter is between two baking sheets.
6. Place into an oven and bake for about 8 minutes until the pizza crust is golden brown.
7. For the toppings, place your ground beef in a sauté pan and fry until its brown and wash your mushrooms very well.
8. After the crust is baked, remove the top layer of parchment paper carefully to prevent the paper from sticking to the pizza crust. Put your toppings on top of the crust and bake for an extra 8 minutes.
9. Once ready, slide the pizza off the parchment paper and into a plate.

Mini Mac in a Bowl

Preparation Time: 5 minutes
Cooking Time: 15 minutes
Servings: 1
Ingredients:

- 5 oz. lean ground beef
- 2 tablespoons diced white or yellow onion.
- 1/8 teaspoon onion powder
- 1/8 teaspoon white vinegar
- 1 oz. dill pickle slices
- 1 teaspoon sesame seed
- 3 cups shredded romaine lettuce
- Cooking spray
- 2 tablespoons reduced-fat shredded cheddar cheese
- 2 tablespoons wish-bone light thousand island as dressing

Directions:

1. Place a lightly greased small skillet on fire to heat.
2. Add your onion to cook for about 2–3 minutes.
3. Next, add the beef and allow it to cook until it is brown.
4. Next, mix your vinegar and onion powder with the dressing.
5. Finally, top the lettuce with the cooked meat and sprinkle cheese on it, add your pickle slices.
6. Drizzle the mixture with the sauce and sprinkle the sesame seeds also. Enjoy!

Lean and Green Chicken Pesto Pasta

Preparation Time: 5 minutes
Cooking Time: 15 minutes
Servings: 1
Ingredients:

- 3 cups raw kale leaves
- 2 tablespoon olive oil
- 2 cups fresh basil

- ¼ teaspoon salt
- 3 tablespoon lemon juice
- 3 garlic cloves
- 2 cups cooked chicken breast
- 1 cup baby spinach
- 6 oz. uncooked chicken pasta
- 3 oz. diced fresh mozzarella
- Basil leaves or red pepper flakes to garnish

Directions:

1. Start by making the pesto, add the kale, lemon juice, basil, garlic cloves, olive oil, and salt to a blender and blend until it is smooth.
2. Add pepper to taste.
3. Cook the pasta and strain off the water. Reserve ¼ cup of the liquid.
4. Get a bowl and mix everything, the cooked pasta, pesto, diced chicken, spinach, mozzarella, and the reserved pasta liquid. Sprinkle the mixture with additional chopped basil or red paper flakes (optional). Enjoy!

Polenta with Seared Pears

Preparation Time: 10 minutes
Cooking Time: 50 minutes
Servings: 1
Ingredients:

- 1 cup water, divided, plus more as needed
- 1/2 cups coarse cornmeal
- 1 tablespoon pure maple syrup
- 1/4 tablespoon molasses
- 1/4 teaspoon ground cinnamon
- 1/2 ripe pears, cored and diced
- 1/4 cup fresh cranberries
- 1/4 teaspoon chopped fresh rosemary leaves

Directions:

1. In a pan, cook 5 cups of water to a simmer. While whisking continuously to avoid clumping, slowly pour in the cornmeal. Cook, often stirring with a heavy spoon, for 30 minutes. The polenta should be thick and creamy. While the polenta cooks, in a saucepan over medium heat, stir together the maple syrup, molasses, the remaining ¼-cup of water, and the cinnamon until combined. Bring it to a simmer. Add the pears and cranberries. Cook for 10 minutes, occasionally stirring, until the pears are tender and start to brown. Remove from the heat. Stir in the rosemary and let the mixture sit for 5 minutes. If it is too thick, add another ¼ cup of water and return to the heat. Top with the cranberry-pear mixture.

Bacon and Cauliflower Mac and Cheese

Preparation Time: 5 minutes
Cooking Time: 20 minutes
Servings: 2
Ingredients:

- 2 strips of bacon
- ½ cup cauliflower florets, chopped
- 3 tablespoons butter, unsalted
- 3 ounces whipped topping
- 3 tablespoons grated cheddar cheese

EXTRA:

- ½ teaspoon salt
- 1/8 teaspoon ground black pepper
- ¼ teaspoon cayenne pepper
- ¾ cup of water

Directions:

1. Take a skillet pan, place it over medium heat and when hot, add bacon and cook for 5 minutes or until crispy.
2. Transfer bacon to a plate, pat dry with paper towels, chop the bacon and set aside until required.
3. When done, drain the cauliflower and then set aside until required.
4. Return saucepan over medium heat, add butter, whipped topping, salt, black pepper, and cayenne pepper, cook for 3 to 5 minutes until the butter has melted and a thick sauce comes together, stirring continuously.
5. Add bacon into the sauce, stir until combined, and remove the pan from heat. Serve straight away.

Taco Stuffed Avocados

Preparation Time: 5 minutes
Cooking Time: 12 minutes
Servings: 1
Ingredients:

- ¼ pound ground turkey
- 2-ounce tomato sauce
- 1 medium avocado, pitted, halved
- ½ cup shredded cheddar cheese
- 2 tablespoon shredded lettuce

EXTRA:

- 1/8 teaspoon garlic powder
- ¼ teaspoon salt
- ½ tablespoon red chili powder

Directions:

1. Take a skillet pan, place it over medium heat, add ground turkey and cook for 5 minutes until nicely golden brown. Reserve the grease for later use, then season the turkey with garlic powder, salt, and red chili powder, stir in tomato sauce and cook for 3 minutes until the meat has thoroughly cooked.
2. Cut the avocado into half, remove its pit and then stuff the crater with prepared meat.
3. Top meat with cheddar cheese and lettuce and serve.

Tuna Cakes

Preparation Time: 5 minutes
Cooking Time: 6 minutes
Servings: 2
Ingredients:

- 5-ounce tuna, packed in water
- 1 tablespoon mustard
- 1 teaspoon garlic powder
- 1 tablespoon coconut oil

EXTRA:

- ¼ teaspoon salt
- 1/8 teaspoon ground black pepper

Directions:

1. Drain the tuna, add it in a medium bowl and break it well with a fork.
2. Then add remaining ingredients, stir until well mixed and then shape the mixture into four patties.
3. Take a medium skillet pan, place it over medium heat, add oil and when hot, add tuna patties and cook for 3 minutes per side until golden brown. Serve patties straight away or serve as a wrap with iceberg lettuce.

Roasted Green Beans

Preparation Time: 5 minutes
Cooking Time: 25 minutes
Servings: 2
Ingredients:

- ½ pound green beans
- ½ cup grated parmesan cheese
- 3 tablespoons coconut oil
- ½ teaspoon garlic powder

EXTRA:

- 1/3 teaspoon salt
- 1/8 teaspoon ground black pepper

Directions:

1. Switch on the oven, then set it to 425°F, and let preheat.

2. Take a baking sheet, line green beans on it, and set aside until required.

3. Prepare the dressing, and for this, place remaining ingredients in a bowl, except for cheese and whisk until combined. Drizzle the dressing over green beans, toss until well coated, and then bake for 20 minutes until green beans are tender-crisp.

4. Then sprinkle cheese on top of beans and continue roasting for 3 to 5 minutes or until cheese melts and nicely golden brown. Serve straight away.

Vegan Alfredo Fettuccine Pasta

Preparation Time: 15 minutes

Cooking Time: 15 minutes

Servings: 1

Ingredients:

- White potatoes - 2 medium
- White onion - ¼
- Italian seasoning - 1 tablespoon
- Lemon juice - 1 teaspoon
- Garlic - 2 cloves
- Salt - 1 teaspoon
- Fettuccine pasta - 12 ounces
- Raw cashew - ½ cup
- Nutritional yeast (optional) - 1 teaspoon
- Truffle oil (optional) - ¼ teaspoon

Directions:

1. Start by placing a pot on high flame and boiling 4 cups of water.

2. Peel the potatoes and cut them into small cubes. Cut the onion into cubes as well.

3. Add the potatoes and onions to the boiling water and cook for about 10 minutes.

4. Remove the onions and potatoes. Keep aside. Save the water.

5. Take another pot and fill it with water. Season generously with salt.

6. Toss in the fettuccine pasta and cook as per package instructions.

7. Take a blender and add in the raw cashews, veggies, nutritional yeast, truffle oil, lemon juice, and 1 cup of the saved water. Blend into a smooth puree. Add in the garlic and salt.

8. Drain the cooked pasta using a colander. Transfer into a mixing bowl.

9. Pour the prepared sauce on top of the cooked fettuccine pasta. Serve.

Spinach Pasta in Pesto Sauce

Preparation Time: 20 minutes

Cooking Time: 15 minutes

Servings: 1

Ingredients:

- Olive oil - 1 tablespoon
- Spinach - 5 ounces
- All-purpose flour - 2 cups
- Salt - 1 tablespoon plus ¼ teaspoon (keep it divided)
- Water - 2 tablespoons
- Roasted vegetable for serving
- Pesto for serving
- Fresh basil for serving

Directions:

1. Take a large pot and fill it with water. Place it over a high flame and bring the water to a boil. Add one tablespoon of salt. While the water is boiling, place a large saucepan over medium flame.

2. Pour in the olive oil and heat it through, toss in the spinach and sauté for 5 minutes.
3. Take a food processor and transfer the wilted spinach. Process until the spinach is fine in texture.
4. Add in the flour bit by bit and continue to process to form a crumbly dough.
5. Further, add ¼ teaspoon of salt and 1 tbsp of water while processing to bring the dough together. Add the remaining 1 tbsp of water if required. Remove the dough onto a flat surface and sprinkle with flour. Knead well to form a dough ball. Use a rolling pin to roll out the dough. The dimensions of the rolled dough should be 18 inches long and 12 inches wide. The thickness should be about ¼ - inch thick.
6. Cut the rolled dough into long and even strips using a pizza cutter. Make sure the strips are ½ - inch wide.
7. The strips need to be rolled into evenly sized thick noodles.
8. Toss in the prepared noodles and cook for about 4 minutes. Drain using a colander.
9. Transfer the noodles into a large mixing bowl and add in the roasted vegetables, pesto. Toss well to combine.
10. Garnish with basil leaves.

Shredded Chicken in a lettuce wrap

Preparation Time: 5 minutes
Cooking Time: 15 minutes
Servings: 2
Ingredients:

- 2 leaves of iceberg lettuce
- 2 large chicken thighs
- 2 tablespoon shredded cheddar cheese

- 3 cups hot water
- 4 tablespoon tomato sauce

EXTRA:
- 1 tablespoon soy sauce
- 1 tablespoon red chili powder
- ¾ teaspoon salt
- ½ teaspoon cracked black pepper

Directions:

1. Switch on the instant pot, place chicken thighs in it, and add remaining ingredients except for lettuce.
2. Stir until just mixed, shut the instant pot with a lid and cook for 15 minutes at high pressure and when done, release the stress naturally.
3. Then open the instant pot, transfer chicken to a cutting board and shred with two forks.
4. Evenly divide the chicken between two lettuce leaves, and drizzle with some of the cooking liquid, reserving the remaining cooking liquid for later use as chicken broth. Serve straight away.

Turkey Lettuce Wraps

Preparation Time: 5 minutes
Cooking Time: 15 minutes
Servings: 2
Ingredients:

- ¼ pound ground turkey
- 2 leaves of iceberg lettuce
- 1 tablespoon sesame oil

- 2 tablespoons soy sauce
- 1 tbsp cheddar cheese

EXTRA:
- 1 teaspoon garlic powder
- 1 teaspoon coconut oil
- ¼ teaspoon salt
- ¼ teaspoon cracked black pepper

Directions:

1. Take a skillet pan, place it over medium heat, add coconut oil and when hot, add turkey and cook for 7 to 10 minutes until nicely browned.
2. Meanwhile, rinse the lettuce leaves and pat dry with a paper towel, set aside until required. Prepare the sauce, and for this, whisk together sesame oil, soy sauce, garlic powder, salt, and black pepper. Pour the sauce into the cooked turkey and continue cooking for 3 minutes or until the sauce has evaporated. Top with cheddar and serve.

Buttery Broccoli and Bacon

Preparation Time: 5 minutes
Cooking Time: 10 minutes
Servings: 2
Ingredients:

- 1 slice of turkey bacon
- 1 cup chopped broccoli florets

- 1/8 teaspoon garlic powder
- ¼ teaspoon Italian seasoning
- ¼ tablespoon unsalted butter

EXTRA:

- 1/8 teaspoon salt
- 1/8 teaspoon ground black pepper

Directions:

1. Take a medium skillet pan, place it over high heat, add bacon slice and cook for 3 to 5 minutes until crispy.
2. Transfer bacon to a cutting board and then chop it into small pieces.
3. Reduce the heat to medium-low level, add broccoli florets into the pan, stir well into the bacon grease, add butter, then toss until mixed and cook for 5 minutes until tender.
4. Season the broccoli florets with salt, black pepper, and Italian seasoning, add chopped bacon, stir well and cook for 2 minutes until thoroughly heated.

Creamy Curry Noodles

Preparation Time: 19 minutes
Cooking Time: 10 minutes
Servings: 4
Ingredients:
CREAMY CURRY SAUCE

- Apple cider vinegar, two tablespoons
- Water, one-quarter of one cup
- Avocado oil, two tablespoons
- Turmeric, ground, one teaspoon
- Black pepper, one half teaspoon
- Tahini, one-quarter of one cup
- Coriander, ground, one- and one-half teaspoons

- Cumin, ground, one teaspoon
- Salt, one teaspoon
- Curry powder, two teaspoons
- Ginger, ground, one quarter teaspoon

NOODLE BOWL

- Cilantro, fresh, chopped small, one half cup
- Bell pepper, red, one cleaned and diced
- Zucchini noodles, one sixteen-ounce pack
- Carrots, two, peeled and cut in julienne strips
- Kale, two cups packed
- Cauliflower, one half of one head chopped small

Directions:

1. Cover the zucchini noodles with two cups of boiling water in a medium-sized bowl and set them off to the side. After leaving the noodles in the water for five minutes, drain off the water and place the noodles back into the bowl. Prep all of the veggies and then toss them into the bowl with the noodles. Toss the ingredients in the bowl gently, but well.
2. Divide the leaves of kale onto four serving plates. Mix the list of ingredients for the Creamy Curry Sauce and blend them until they are smooth and creamy. When the sauce is well mixed, then pour it over the ingredients in the bowl and toss the ingredients well until all are covered with the sauce.
3. Then divide the noodles over the kale on the four plates and serve.

Roasted Vegetables

Preparation Time: 10 minutes
Cooking Time: 20 minutes
Servings: 4
Ingredients:

- Cilantro, chopped, one-quarter of one cup
- Green onion, diced, one half of one cup

MASALA SEASONING

- Black pepper, one half teaspoon
- Turmeric, one quarter teaspoon
- Chili powder, ground, one half teaspoon
- Tomato puree, one half of one cup
- Garam masala, one quarter teaspoon

- Salt, one half teaspoon
- Garlic, minced, one tablespoon
- Olive oil, two tablespoons
- Ginger, ground, two teaspoons

VEGGIES

- Cauliflower, one cup in small pieces
- Mushrooms, sliced one half of one cup
- Green beans, three-fourths of one cup

Directions:

1. Heat the oven to 400. Place the rack in the oven in the middle. Use aluminum foil or parchment paper to cover a baking sheet completely. Chop the veggies if they are not already chopped. Use a medium-sized bowl to mix the chili powder, ginger, garam masala, garlic, pepper, salt, and the tomato puree, making sure the ingredients are all mixed well.
2. Then mix in the olive oil. Place the chopped veggies into this mixture and mix them in well. Then place the coated veggies onto the covered baking sheet in one single layer.
3. Roast the veggies in the heated oven for thirty to forty minutes or until the veggies are cooked in a manner in which you like them.

Green Pea Fritter

Preparation Time: 10 minutes
Cooking Time: 20 minutes
Servings: 4
Ingredients:

- Frozen peas, two cups
- Olive oil, one tablespoon + one tablespoon
- Onion, one diced
- Garlic, three tablespoons

- Chickpea flour, one- and one-half cups
- Baking soda, one teaspoon
- Salt, one quarter teaspoon
- Rosemary, one teaspoon
- Thyme, one half teaspoon
- Marjoram, one teaspoon
- Lemon juice, two tablespoons

Directions:

1. Heat the oven to 350°F. Use spray oil to spray a baking sheet. Boil the peas for five minutes.
2. Pour one tablespoon of olive oil in a skillet and fry the garlic and onion for five minutes.
3. Pour the garlic and onion with the olive oil in a bowl and add the cooked peas, mashing them until they make a thick paste. Blend in the marjoram, thyme, rosemary, salt, baking soda, and chickpea flour.
4. Dampen your hands and form the mash into ten equal-sized patties. Brush the patties with the other tablespoon of olive oil. Bake them for 18 minutes in the oven, turning them over after 9 minutes. Serve immediately!

Roasted Mushrooms and Shallots

Preparation Time: 10 minutes
Cooking Time: 20 minutes
Servings: 4
Ingredients:

- Mushrooms, fresh, one-pound cut into bite-size pieces

- Shallots, two cups sliced thick
- Olive oil, two tablespoons
- Thyme, dried, one teaspoon
- Salt, one quarter teaspoon
- Black pepper, one quarter teaspoon
- Red wine vinegar, one third cup

Directions:
1. Preheat your oven to 450°F.
2. Place the shallots and mushrooms in a large bowl and add salt, pepper, thyme, and olive oil and toss the ingredients together to coat the shallots and mushrooms thoroughly.
3. Roast the veggies on a baking sheet for fifteen minutes. Pour the red wine vinegar over the veggies and bake for five more minutes.

Garlic Chili Roasted Kohlrabi
Preparation Time: 5 minutes
Cooking Time: 12 minutes
Servings: 1
Ingredients:
- Olive oil, two tablespoons
- Garlic, minced, one tablespoon
- Chili pepper, one teaspoon
- Salt, one quarter teaspoon
- Kohlrabi, one and one-half pounds, peel and cut into one half inch wedges
- Cilantro, fresh, chopped, two tablespoons

Directions:
1. Heat your oven to 450°F. Mix in a large bowl, the pepper, salt, chili pepper, garlic, and olive oil. Put in the kohlrabi and toss well to coat the kohlrabi.
2. Bake the coated kohlrabi for twenty minutes, stirring it around when you are about halfway done with cooking. Sprinkle on the cilantro and serve.

Vegetarian Nachos
Preparation Time: 15 minutes
Cooking Time: 0 minutes
Servings: 6
Ingredients:
- Pita chips, whole wheat, three cups
- Nutritional yeast, one half cup
- Oregano, dried, one tablespoon minced
- Romaine lettuce, one cup chopped
- Grape tomatoes, one-half cup cut in quarters
- Olive oil, two tablespoons
- Lemon juice, one tablespoon
- Hummus, one-third cup prepared
- Black pepper, one half teaspoon
- Red onion, two tablespoons minced
- Tofu, one-half cup cut into small crumbles
- Black olives, two tablespoons chopped

Directions:
1. Mix the hummus, pepper, olive oil, and lemon juice in a mixing bowl. Spread a layer of the pita chips on a serving platter.
2. Drizzle three-fourths of the hummus mix over the pita chips. Use the lettuce, red onion, tomatoes, and olives to garnish the hummus.
3. Make a small mound of the leftover hummus in the middle of the chips, then garnish all with the oregano and the nutritional yeast.

VEGAN Macaroni and Cheese
Preparation Time: 15 minutes
Cooking Time: 20 minutes
Servings: 4
Ingredients:
- Elbow macaroni, whole grain, eight ounces, cooked
- Nutritional yeast, one quarter cup
- Garlic, minced, two tablespoons
- Apple cider vinegar, two teaspoons
- Broccoli, one head with florets cut into bite-sized pieces

- Water, one cup (more if needed)
- Garlic powder, one half teaspoon
- Avocado oil, two tablespoons
- Red pepper, flakes, one eighth teaspoon
- Onion, yellow, chopped, one cup
- Salt, one half teaspoon
- Russet potato, peeled and grated, one cup (about two small potatoes)
- Dry mustard powder, one half teaspoon
- Onion powder, one half teaspoon

Directions:

1. Cook the broccoli for five minutes in boiling water. Add the cooked broccoli to the cooked pasta in a large mixing bowl.
2. Cook the onion in the avocado oil for five minutes, then stir in the red pepper flakes, garlic, salt, mustard powder, garlic powder, grated potato, and onion powder. Cook this for three minutes and then pour in the water and mix well. Cook this for eight to ten minutes or until the potatoes are soft.
3. Pour all of this mixture carefully into a blender and add in the nutritional yeast and the vinegar and then blend. When this is creamy and smooth, then pour it into the mixing bowl and mix well with the broccoli and pasta.

Cilantro Lime Coleslaw

Preparation Time: 5 minutes
Cooking Time: 0 minutes
Servings: 5
Ingredients:

- Avocados, two
- Garlic, minced, one tablespoon
- Coleslaw, ready-made in a bag, fourteen ounces
- Cilantro, fresh leaves, one-quarter cup minced
- Salt, one half teaspoon
- Lime juice, two tablespoons
- Water, one quarter cup

Directions:

1. Except for the slaw mix, put all of the ingredients that are listed into a blender. Blend these ingredients well until they are creamy and smooth.
2. Mix the coleslaw mix in with this dressing and then toss it gently to mix it well.
3. Keep the mixed coleslaw in the refrigerator until you are ready to serve.

Delicious Broccoli

Preparation Time: 15 minutes
Cooking Time: 15 minutes
Servings: 8
Ingredients:

- 2 oranges, sliced in half
- 1 lb. broccoli rabe
- 2 tablespoons sesame oil, toasted
- Salt and pepper to taste
- 1 tablespoon sesame seeds, toasted

Directions:

1. Pour the oil into a pan over medium heat.
2. Add the oranges and cook until caramelized and transfer to a plate.
3. Put the broccoli in the pan and cook for 8 minutes.
4. Squeeze the oranges to release juice in a bowl, add oil, salt, and pepper and coat the broccoli rabe with the mixture. Sprinkle seeds on top.

Spicy Peanut Soba Noodles

Preparation Time: 7 minutes
Cooking Time: 17 minutes
Servings: 1

Ingredients:

- 5 ounces uncooked soba noodles
- ½ tablespoon low sodium soy sauce

- 1 clove garlic, minced
- 4 teaspoons water
- 1 small head broccoli, cut into florets
- ½ cup carrot
- ¼ cup finely chopped scallions
- 3 tablespoons peanut butter

- 1 tablespoon honey
- 1 teaspoon crushed red pepper flakes
- 2 teaspoons vegetable oil
- 4 ounces button mushrooms, discard stems
- 3 tablespoons peanuts, dry roasted, unsalted

Directions:

1. Cook soba noodles following the directions on the package.
2. Add peanut butter, honey, water, soy sauce, garlic, and red pepper flakes. Whisk until well combined.
3. Place a skillet over medium heat. Add oil. When the oil is heated, add broccoli and sauté for a few minutes until crisp as well as tender. Add mushrooms and sauté until the mushrooms are tender. Turn off the heat.
4. Add the sauce mixture and carrots and mix well.
5. Crush the peanuts by rolling with a rolling pin.
6. Divide the noodles into bowls. Pour sauce mixture over it. Sprinkle scallions and peanuts on top and serve.

Dinner Recipes

Garlic Zucchini and Cauliflower

Preparation Time: 10 minutes
Cooking Time: 20 minutes
Servings: 4
Ingredients:

- 4 zucchinis, cut into medium fries
- 1 cup cauliflower florets
- 1 tablespoon capers, drained
- Juice of ½ lemon
- A pinch of salt and black pepper
- ½ teaspoon chili powder
- 1 tablespoon olive oil
- ¼ teaspoon garlic powder

Directions:

1. Spread the zucchini fries on a lined baking sheet, add the rest of the ingredients, toss, introduce in the oven, bake at 400 degrees F for 20 minutes, divide between plates and serve.

Garlic Beans

Preparation Time: 10 minutes
Cooking Time: 10 minutes
Servings: 4
Ingredients:

- Juice of 1 lemon
- Zest of 1 lemon, grated
- 2 tablespoons avocado oil
- 4 garlic cloves, minced
- ½ teaspoon turmeric powder
- 1 teaspoon garam masala
- 1 red onion, sliced
- 1 yellow bell pepper, sliced
- 10 ounces green beans, halved
- A pinch of black pepper

Directions:

1. Heat up a pan with the oil over medium-high heat, add the garlic and onion and cook for 2 minutes.
2. Add green beans and the other ingredients, toss, cook for 8 minutes, divide between plates and serve.

Mustard Beets

Preparation Time: 10 minutes
Cooking Time: 0 minutes
Servings: 4
Ingredients:

- 1 tablespoon Dijon mustard
- 1 and ½ tablespoon olive oil
- 8 ounces beets, cooked and sliced
- 1 teaspoon garam masala
- 1 teaspoon coriander, ground
- 1 teaspoon basil, dried
- A pinch of black pepper

Directions:

1. In a bowl, mix the beets with the oil, mustard and the other ingredients, toss and serve.

Parsley Green Beans

Preparation Time: 10 minutes
Cooking Time: 20 minutes
Servings: 6
Ingredients:

- 3 tablespoons olive oil
- 3 pounds green beans, halved
- A pinch of salt and black pepper
- 2 tablespoons balsamic vinegar
- 2 yellow onions, chopped
- 2 and ½ tablespoons parsley, chopped

Directions:

1. Heat a pan with the oil over medium heat, add the green beans and the other ingredients, toss, cook for 20 minutes, divide between plates and serve.

Squash and Tomatoes

Preparation Time: 15 minutes
Cooking Time: 12 minutes
Servings: 2
Ingredients:

- 8 oz yellow squash, peeled and roughly cubed
- 1 cup cherry tomatoes, halved

- 3 tablespoons tomato sauce
- 1 teaspoon sweet paprika
- 1 teaspoon coriander, ground
- 1 teaspoon oregano, dried
- 1 teaspoon olive oil
- 1 teaspoon white pepper

Directions:

1. Heat up a pan with the oil over medium heat, add the squash, tomatoes and the other ingredients.
2. Cook for 12 minutes on low heat.
3. Transfer into plates and serve.

Bok Choy Salad

Preparation Time: 10 minutes
Cooking Time: 10 minutes
Servings: 5
Ingredients:

- 10 oz bok choy, chopped
- 1 cup cherry tomatoes, halved

- 1 tablespoon black olives, pitted and sliced
- 1 mango, peeled and cubed
- Juice of ½ orange
- 1 teaspoon curry powder
- 1 teaspoon sesame oil
- 1 tablespoon lemon juice

Directions:

1. Heat up a pan with the oil over medium-high heat, add the bok choy, tomatoes and the other ingredients, toss and cook for 10 minutes.
2. Divide into bowls and serve cold.

Balsamic Arugula and Beets

Preparation Time: 10 minutes
Cooking Time: 0 minutes
Servings: 4
Ingredients:

- 2 cups baby arugula
- 1 tablespoon balsamic vinegar

- 1 teaspoon olive oil
- 2 red beets, baked, peeled and cubed
- 1 avocado, peeled, pitted and cubed
- 1 teaspoon marsala
- ½ teaspoon salt
- ½ teaspoon cayenne pepper

Directions:

1. In a bowl, mix the arugula with the beets and the vinegar. Mix and add olive oil, chopped avocado and marsala, salt and pepper. Mix well.
2. Serve and enjoy.

Herbed Beets

Preparation Time: 10 minutes
Cooking Time: 40 minutes
Servings: 3

Ingredients:

- 2 big red beets, peeled and roughly cubed

- 1 tablespoon chives, chopped
- 1 tablespoon cilantro, chopped
- 1 tablespoon basil, chopped
- Juice of 1 lime
- A pinch of salt and black pepper

- ¼ teaspoon dried oregano
- ¼ teaspoon ground nutmeg
- ¼ teaspoon ground cumin
- 1 tablespoon olive oil

Directions:

1. Preheat oven to 400°F. Take a baking dish with parchment paper.
2. Take a bowl and place in the chives, cilantro and beets. Add basil, salt, pepper and lime juice and mix well. Add sprinkle the oregano, nutmeg, and cumin. Pour a tablespoon of olive oil and mix well.
3. Transfer in the baking dish and bake for 40 minutes.
4. Divide between plates and serve.

Marinara Broccoli

Preparation Time: 10 minutes
Cooking Time: 15 minutes
Servings: 4
Ingredients:

- 2 cups broccoli florets
- 1 teaspoon sweet paprika
- 1 teaspoon coriander, ground

- ¼ cup marinara sauce
- ½ teaspoon ground black pepper
- ½ teaspoon salt
- ½ teaspoon garlic powder
- 1 teaspoon olive oil
- Juice of 1 lime

Directions:

1. In a roasting pan, mix the broccoli with the marinara and the other ingredients, toss and bake at 400 degrees F for 15 minutes. Divide between plates and serve.

Spinach and Pear Salad

Preparation Time: 10 minutes
Cooking Time: 0 minutes
Servings: 2
Ingredients:

- 1 bell pepper, chopped
- ½ cup radishes, halved
- ½ cup cherry tomatoes, halved
- 2 cups baby spinach
- 2 pears, cored and cut into wedges
- 1 tablespoon walnuts, chopped
- 1 teaspoon chives, chopped
- A pinch of salt and black pepper
- Juice of 1 lime

Directions:

1. In a bowl, mix the radishes with the pepper, tomatoes and the other ingredients. Serve and enjoy!

Olives and Mango Mix

Preparation Time: 10 minutes
Cooking Time: 0 minutes
Servings: 2

Ingredients:

- 1 cup black olives, pitted and halved
- 1 cup kalamata olives, pitted and halved

- 1 cup mango, peeled and cubed
- A pinch of salt and black pepper
- Juice of 1 lime
- 1 teaspoon sweet paprika
- 1 teaspoon coriander, ground
- 1 tablespoon olive oil

Directions:

1. In a bowl mix the olives with the mango and the other ingredients, toss and serve.

Eggplant and Avocado Mix

Preparation Time: 10 minutes

Cooking Time: 20 minutes

Servings: 4

Ingredients:

- 1-pound eggplant, roughly cubed
- 2 avocados, peeled, pitted and cubed
- 1 red onion, chopped
- 1 teaspoon curry powder
- Juice of 1 lime
- ½ cup crushed tomatoes
- 1 tablespoon olive oil
- 1 teaspoon salt
- 1 teaspoon chili powder

Directions:

1. Heat up a pan with the oil over medium heat, add the onion and cook for 5 minutes.
2. Add the eggplants, avocados and the other ingredients, toss and cook for 15 minutes more.
3. Divide between plates and serve.

Red Onion, Avocado and Radishes Mix

Preparation Time: 15 minutes

Cooking Time: 12 minutes

Servings: 2

Ingredients:

- 2 red onions, peeled and sliced
- 2 avocados, peeled, pitted and sliced
- 1 cup radishes, halved
- 1 teaspoon oregano, dried
- 1 teaspoon basil, dried
- 1 tablespoon olive oil
- 1 teaspoon lemon juice
- ¼ teaspoon salt

Directions:

1. Heat a pan with the oil over medium heat, add the onions, oregano and basil and cook for 5 minutes.
2. Add the rest of the ingredients, toss, cook for 7 minutes more, divide into bowls and serve.

Cajun and Balsamic Okra

Preparation Time: 10 minutes

Cooking Time: 15 minutes

Servings: 2

Ingredients:

- 1 cup okra, sliced
- ½ cup crushed tomatoes
- 1 teaspoon Cajun seasoning
- 2 tablespoons balsamic vinegar
- 1 teaspoon salt
- 1 teaspoon ground black pepper
- 1 tablespoon fresh parsley, chopped
- 1 teaspoon olive oil

Directions:

1. Heat up a pan with the oil over medium heat, add the okra, seasoning and the remaining ingredients, toss and cook for 15 minutes. Divide into bowls and serve.

Cashew Zucchinis

Preparation Time: 10 minutes

Cooking Time: 40 minutes

Servings: 4

Ingredients:

- 1-pound zucchinis, sliced
- ½ cup cashews, soaked for a couple of hours and drained
- 1 cup coconut milk
- ¼ teaspoon nutmeg, ground
- 1 teaspoon chili powder
- A pinch of salt and black pepper

Directions:

1.In a roasting pan, mix the zucchinis with the cashews and the other ingredients, toss gently and cook at 380 degrees F for 40 minutes.

2.Divide into bowls and serve.

Shaved Brussel Sprout Salad

Preparation Time: 40 minutes

Cooking Time: 15 minutes

Servings: 4

Ingredients:

DRESSING:

- 1 tbsp. brown mustard
- 1 tbsp. maple syrup
- 2 tbsp. apple cider vinegar
- 2 tbsp. extra virgin olive oil
- ½ tbsp. garlic minced

SALAD:

- ½ cup dry red kidney beans
- ¼ cup dry chickpeas
- 2 cups Brussel sprouts
- 1 cup purple onion
- 1 small sour apple
- ½ cup slivered almonds, crushed
- ½ cup walnuts, crushed
- ½ cup cranberries, dried
- ¼ tsp Salt
- ¼ tsp pepper

Directions:

1. Take a pot and bring the water to a boil. Season with salt and add beans. Cook them on medium for 15 minutes.
2. Combine all dressing ingredients in a bowl and stir well until combined.
3. Refrigerate the dressing for up to one hour before serving.
4. Using a grater, mandolin, or knife to slice each Brussel sprout thinly. Repeat this with the apple and onion.
5. Take a large bowl to mix the chickpeas, beans, sprouts, apples, onions, cranberries, and nuts.
6. Drizzle the cold dressing over the salad to coat. Serve with salt and pepper to taste!

Colorful Protein Power Salad

Preparation Time: 30 minutes

Cooking Time: 20 minutes

Servings: 2

Ingredients:

- ½ cup dry quinoa
- 2 cups dry navy beans
- 1 green onion, chopped
- 2 tsp. garlic, minced
- 3 cups green or purple cabbage, chopped
- 4 cups kale, fresh or frozen, chopped

- 1 cup shredded carrot, chopped
- 2 tbsp. extra virgin olive oil
- 1 tsp. lemon juice
- ¼ tsp Salt
- ¼ tsp pepper

Directions:
1. Take a pot and bring the water to a boil. Season with salt and add quinoa. Cook them on medium for 5 minutes
2. Take a pot and bring the water to a boil. Season with salt and add beans. Cook them on medium for 15 minutes
3. Heat 1 tablespoon of the olive oil in a frying pan over medium heat.
4. Add the chopped green onion, garlic, and cabbage, and sauté for 2-3 minutes.
5. Add the kale, the remaining 1 tablespoon of olive oil, and salt. Lower the heat and cover until the greens have wilted, around 5 minutes. Remove the pan from the stove and set aside.
6. Take a large bowl and mix the remaining ingredients with the kale and cabbage mixture once it has cooled down. Add more salt and pepper to taste. Mix until everything is distributed evenly. Serve topped with a dressing.

Edamame and Ginger Citrus Salad

Preparation Time: 25 minutes
Cooking Time: 15 minutes
 Servings: 3
Ingredients:
DRESSING:

- ¼ cup orange juice
- 1 tsp. lime juice
- ½ tbsp. maple syrup
- ½ tsp. ginger, finely minced
- ½ tbsp. sesame oil

SALAD:

- ½ cup dry green lentils
- 2 cups carrots, shredded
- 4 cups kale, fresh or frozen, chopped
- 1 cup edamame, shelled
- 1 tablespoon roasted sesame seeds
- 2 tsp. mint, chopped
- Salt and pepper to taste
- 1 small avocado, peeled, pitted, diced

Directions:
1. Take a pot and bring the water to a boil. Season with salt and add lentils. Cook them on medium for 15 minutes.
2. Combine the orange and lime juices, maple syrup, and ginger in a small bowl. Mix with a whisk while slowly adding the sesame oil. Add the cooked lentils, carrots, kale, edamame, sesame seeds, and mint to a large bowl.
3. Add the dressing and stir well until all the ingredients are coated evenly.
4. Serve topped with avocado and an additional sprinkle of mint.

Taco Tempeh Salad

Preparation Time: 25 minutes
Cooking Time: 0 minutes
Servings: 3
Ingredients:

- 1 cup dry black beans
- 1 8-oz. package tempeh
- 1 tbsp. lime or lemon juice
- 2 tbsp. extra virgin olive oil
- 1 tsp. maple syrup

- ½ tsp. chili powder
- ¼ tsp. cumin
- ¼ tsp. paprika
- 1 large bunch of kale, fresh or frozen, chopped
- 1 large avocado, peeled, pitted, diced
- ½ cup salsa
- ¼ tsp Salt
- ¼ tsp pepper

Directions:
1. Take a pot and bring the water to a boil. Season with salt and add beans. Cook them on medium for 15 minutes

2. Cut the tempeh into ¼-inch cubes, place in a bowl, and then add the lime or lemon juice, 1 tablespoon of olive oil, maple syrup, chili powder, cumin, and paprika.
3. Stir well and let the tempeh marinate in the fridge for at least 1 hour, up to 12 hours.
4. Heat the remaining 1 tablespoon of olive oil in a frying pan over medium heat.
5. Add the marinated tempeh mixture and cook until brown and crispy on both sides, around 10 minutes.
6. Put the chopped kale in a bowl with the cooked beans and prepared tempeh.
7. Store, or serve the salad immediately, topped with salsa, avocado, and salt and pepper to taste.

Lebanese Potato Salad

Preparation Time: 5 minutes
Cooking Time: 10 minutes
Servings: 4
Ingredients:

- 1-pound Russet potatoes
- 1 ½ tablespoons extra virgin olive oil
- 2 scallions, thinly sliced
- Freshly ground pepper to taste
- 2 tablespoons lemon juice
- ¼ teaspoon salt or to taste
- 2 tablespoons fresh mint leaves, chopped

Directions:

1. Place a saucepan half filled with water over medium heat. Add salt and potatoes and cook for 10 minutes until tender. Drain the potatoes and place in a bowl of cold water. When cool enough to handle, peel and cube the potatoes. Place in a bowl.

To make dressing:

2. Add oil, lemon juice, salt and pepper in a bowl and whisk well. Drizzle dressing over the potatoes. Toss well.
3. Add scallions and mint and toss well.
4. Divide into 4 plates and serve.

Chickpea and Spinach Salad

Preparation Time: 5 minutes
Cooking Time: 0 minutes
Servings: 4
Ingredients:

- 2 cans (14.5 ounces each) chickpeas, drained, rinsed
- 7 ounces vegan feta cheese, crumbled or chopped
- 1 tablespoon lemon juice
- 1/3 -½ cup olive oil
- ½ teaspoon salt or to taste
- 4-6 cups spinach, torn
- ½ cup raisins
- 2 tablespoons honey
- 1-2 teaspoons ground cumin
- 1 teaspoon chili flakes

Directions:

1. Add cheese, chickpeas and spinach into a large bowl.
2. To make dressing: Add rest of the ingredients into another bowl and mix well.
3. Pour dressing over the salad. Toss well and serve.

Italian Veggie Salad

Preparation Time: 10 minutes
Cooking Time: 0 minutes
Servings: 8
Ingredients:
FOR SALAD:

- 1 cup fresh baby carrots, quartered lengthwise
- 1 celery rib, sliced
- 3 large mushrooms, thinly sliced
- 1 cup cauliflower florets, bite sized, blanched

- 1 cup broccoli florets, blanched
- 1 cup thinly sliced radish
- 4-5 ounces hearts of romaine salad mix to serve

FOR DRESSING:

- ½ package Italian salad dressing mix

- 3 tablespoons white vinegar
- 3 tablespoons water
- 3 tablespoons olive oil
- 3-4 pepperoncino, chopped

Directions:

To make salad:

1. Add all the ingredients of the salad except hearts of romaine to a bowl and toss.

To make dressing:

2. Add all the ingredients of the dressing in a small bowl. Whisk well.
3. Pour dressing over salad and toss well. Refrigerate for a couple of hours.
4. Place romaine in a large bowl. Place the chilled salad over it and serve.

Wasabi Tuna Asian Salad

Preparation Time: 30 minutes
Cooking Time: 10 minutes
Servings: 1
Ingredients:

- Lime juice (1 teaspoon)
- Non-stick cooking spray

- Pepper/dash of salt
- Wasabi paste (1 teaspoon)
- Olive oil (2 teaspoons)
- Chopped or shredded cucumbers (1/2 cup)
- Bok Choy stalks (1 cup)
- Raw tuna steak (8 oz.)

Directions:

1. Fish: preheat your skillet to medium heat. Mix your wasabi and lime juice; coat the tuna steaks.
2. Use a non-stick cooking spray on your skillet for 10 seconds.
3. Put your tuna steaks on the skillet and cook over medium heat until you get the desired doneness.
4. Salad: Slice the cucumber into match-stick tiny sizes. Cut the bok Choy into minute pieces. Toss gently with pepper, salt, and olive oil if you want. Enjoy!

Lemon Greek Salad

Preparation Time: 25 minutes
Cooking Time: 25 minutes
Servings: 1
Ingredients:

- Chicken breast (140 oz)
- Chopped cucumber (1 cup)
- Chopped orange/red bell pepper (1 cup)

- Wedged/sliced/chopped tomatoes (1 cup)
- Chopped olives (1/4 cup)
- Fresh parsley (2 tablespoons), finely chopped.
- Finely chopped red onion (2 tablespoons)
- Lemon juice (5 teaspoons)
- Olive oil (1 teaspoon)
- Minced garlic (1 clove)

Directions:

1. Preheat your grill to medium heat.
2. Grill the chicken and cook on each side until the chicken is no longer pink or for 5 minutes.
3. Cut the chicken into tiny pieces. In your serving bowl, mix garlic, olives, and parsley. Whisk in olive oil (1 teaspoon) and lemon juice (4 teaspoons). Add onion, tomatoes, bell pepper, and cucumber.
4. Toss gently. Coat the ingredients with dressing. Add another teaspoon of lemon juice to taste. Divide the salad into two servings and put 6oz chicken on top of each salad. Enjoy!

Potato Carrot Salad

Preparation Time: 4 hours 15 minutes

Cooking Time: 10 minutes

Servings: 1

Ingredients:

- Water
- 1 potato, sliced into cubes
- 1/2 carrots, cut into cubes
- 1/6 tablespoon milk
- 1/6 tablespoon Dijon mustard
- 1/24 cup mayonnaise
- Pepper to taste
- 1/3 teaspoons fresh thyme, chopped
- 1/6 stalk celery, chopped
- 1/6 scallions, chopped
- 1/6 slice turkey bacon, cooked crispy and crumbled

Directions:

1. Fill your pot with water and place it over medium-high heat.
2. Boil the potatoes and carrots for 10 to 12 minutes or until tender. Drain and let cool.
3. In a bowl, mix the milk, mustard, mayonnaise, pepper, and thyme.
4. Stir in the potatoes, carrots, and celery.
5. Coat evenly with the sauce.
6. Cover and refrigerate for 4 hours.
7. Top with the scallions and turkey bacon bits before serving.

Marinated Veggie Salad

Preparation Time: 4 hours and 30 minutes

Cooking Time: 3 minutes

Servings: 1

Ingredients:

- 1 zucchini, sliced
- 4 tomatoes, sliced into wedges
- ¼ cup red onion, sliced thinly
- 1 green bell pepper, sliced
- 2 tablespoons fresh parsley, chopped
- 2 tablespoons red-wine vinegar
- 2 tablespoons olive oil
- 1 clove garlic, minced
- 1 teaspoon dried basil
- 2 tablespoons water
- Pine nuts, toasted and chopped

Directions:

1. In a bowl, combine the zucchini, tomatoes, red onion, green bell pepper, and parsley.
2. Pour the vinegar and oil into a glass jar with a lid. Add the garlic, basil, and water. Seal the jar and stir well to combine. Pour the dressing into the vegetable mixture. Cover the bowl.
3. Marinate in the refrigerator for 4 hours.
4. Garnish with the pine nuts before serving.

Seafood

Baked Cod Crusted with Herbs

Preparation Time: 5 minutes
Cooking Time: 10 minutes
Servings: 4
Ingredients:

- ¼ cup honey
- ¼ teaspoon salt
- ½ cup panko
- ½ teaspoon pepper
- 1 tablespoon extra-virgin olive oil
- 1 tablespoon lemon juice
- 1 teaspoon dried basil
- 1 teaspoon dried parsley
- 1 teaspoon rosemary
- 4 pieces of 4-oz cod fillets

Directions:

1. With olive oil, grease a 9 x 13-inch baking pan and preheat oven to 375°F.
2. In a zip top bag mix panko, rosemary, salt, pepper, parsley and basil.
3. Evenly spread cod fillets in prepped dish and drizzle with lemon juice. Then brush the fillets with honey on all sides. Discard remaining honey if any. Then evenly divide the panko mixture on top of cod fillets.
4. Pop in the oven and bake for ten minutes or until fish is cooked. Serve and enjoy.

Coconut Salsa on Chipotle Fish Tacos

Preparation Time: 10 minutes
Cooking Time: 10 minutes
Servings: 4
Ingredients:

- ¼ cup chopped fresh cilantro
- ½ cup seeded and finely chopped plum tomato
- 1 cup peeled and finely chopped mango
- 1 lime cut into wedges
- 1 tablespoon chipotle Chile powder
- 1 tablespoon safflower oil
- 1/3 cup finely chopped red onion
- 10 tablespoon fresh lime juice, divided
- 4 6-oz boneless, skinless cod fillets
- 5 tablespoon dried unsweetened shredded coconut
- 8 pcs of 6-inch tortillas, heated

Directions:

1. Whisk well Chile powder, oil, and 4 tablespoon lime juice in a glass baking dish. Add cod and marinate for 12 – 15 minutes. Turning once halfway through the marinating time.
2. Make the salsa by mixing coconut, 6 tablespoon lime juice, cilantro, onions, tomatoes and mangoes in a medium bowl. Set aside.
3. On high, heat a grill pan. Place cod and grill for four minutes per side turning only once. Once cooked, slice cod into large flakes and evenly divide onto tortilla. Divide salsa on top of cod and serve with a side of lime wedges.

Creamy Bacon-Fish Chowder

Preparation Time: 10 minutes
Cooking Time: 30 minutes
Servings: 8
Ingredients:

- 1 1/2 lbs. cod
- 1 1/2 teaspoon dried thyme
- 1 large onion, chopped
- 1 medium carrot, coarsely chopped
- 1 tablespoon butter, cut into small pieces
- 1 teaspoon salt, divided
- 3 1/2 cups baking potato, peeled and cubed
- 3 slices uncooked bacon
- 3/4 teaspoon ground black pepper, divided
- 4 1/2 cups water
- 4 bay leaves

- 4 cups 2% reduced-fat milk

Directions:

1. In a large skillet, add the water and bay leaves and let it simmer. Add the fish. Cover and let it simmer some more until the flesh flakes easily with fork. Remove the fish from the skillet and cut into large pieces. Set aside the cooking liquid.
2. Place Dutch oven in medium heat and cook the bacon until crisp. Remove the bacon and reserve the bacon drippings. Crush the bacon and set aside.
3. Stir potato, onion and carrot in the pan with the bacon drippings, cook over medium heat for 10 minutes. Add the cooking liquid, bay leaves, 1/2 teaspoon salt, 1/4 teaspoon pepper and thyme, let it boil. Lower the heat and let simmer for 11 minutes. Add the milk and butter, simmer until the potatoes becomes tender, but do not boil. Add the fish, 1/2 teaspoon salt, 1/2 teaspoon pepper. Remove the bay leaves.
4. Serve sprinkled with the crushed bacon.

Crazy Saganaki Shrimp

Preparation Time: 10 minutes
Cooking Time: 10 minutes
Servings: 4
Ingredients:

- ¼ teaspoon salt
- ½ cup Chardonnay
- ½ cup crumbled Greek feta cheese

- 1 medium bulb. fennel, cored and finely chopped
- 1 small Chile pepper, seeded and minced
- 1 tablespoon extra-virgin olive oil
- 12 jumbo shrimps, deveined with tails left on
- 2 tablespoon lemon juice, divided
- 5 scallions sliced thinly
- Pepper to taste

Directions:

1. In medium bowl, mix salt, lemon juice and shrimp.
2. On medium fire, place a saganaki pan (or large nonstick saucepan) and heat oil.
3. Sauté Chile pepper, scallions, and fennel for 4 minutes or until starting to brown and is already soft. Add wine and sauté for another minute. Place shrimps on top of fennel, cover and cook for 4 minutes or until shrimps are pink.
4. Remove just the shrimp and transfer to a plate.
5. Add pepper, feta and 1 tablespoon lemon juice to pan and cook for a minute or until cheese begins to melt.
6. To serve, place cheese and fennel mixture on a serving plate and top with shrimps.

Cajun Garlic Shrimp Noodle Bowl

Preparation Time: 10 minutes
Cooking Time: 15 minutes
Servings: 2
Ingredients:

- ½ teaspoon salt
- 1 onion, sliced
- 1 red pepper, sliced
- 1 tablespoon butter
- 1 teaspoon garlic granules

- 1 teaspoon onion powder
- 1 teaspoon paprika
- 2 large zucchinis, cut into noodle strips
- 20 jumbo shrimps, shells removed and deveined
- 3 cloves garlic, minced
- 3 tablespoon ghee
- A dash of cayenne pepper
- A dash of red pepper flakes

Directions:

1. Prepare the Cajun seasoning by mixing the onion powder, garlic granules, pepper flakes, cayenne pepper, paprika and salt. Toss in the shrimp to coat in the seasoning.

2. In a skillet, heat the ghee and sauté the garlic, then add red pepper and onions and sauté for 4 minutes.
3. Add the Cajun shrimp and cook until opaque. Set aside.
4. In another pan, heat the butter and sauté the zucchini noodles for three minutes.
5. Assemble by the placing the Cajun shrimps on top of the zucchini noodles.

Cucumber-Basil Salsa on Halibut Pouches

Preparation Time: 10 minutes

Cooking Time: 17 minutes

Servings: 4

Ingredients:

- 1 lime, thinly sliced into 8 pieces
- 2 cups mustard greens, stems removed
- 2 teaspoon olive oil
- 4 – 5 radishes trimmed and quartered
- 44-oz skinless halibut filets

- 4 large fresh basil leaves
- Cayenne pepper to taste – optional
- Pepper and salt to taste

SALSA:

- 1 ½ cups diced cucumber
- 1 ½ finely chopped fresh basil leaves
- 2 teaspoon fresh lime juice
- Pepper and salt to taste

Directions:

1. Preheat oven to 400°F. Prepare parchment papers by making 4 pieces of 15 x 12-inch rectangles. Lengthwise, fold in half and unfold pieces on the table.
2. Season halibut fillets with pepper, salt and pepper. Just to the right of the fold, place ½ cup of mustard greens. Add a basil leaf on center of mustard greens and topped with 1 lime slice. Around the greens, layer ¼ of the radishes. Drizzle with ½ teaspoon of oil, season with pepper and salt. Top it with a slice of halibut fillet.
3. Just as you would make a calzone, fold parchment paper over your filling and crimp the edges of the parchment paper beginning from one end to the other end. To seal the end of the crimped parchment paper, pinch it.
4. Repeat process to remaining ingredients until you have 4 pieces of parchment papers filled with halibut and greens. Place pouches in a pan and bake in the oven until halibut is flaky, around 15 to 17 minutes.
5. While waiting for halibut pouches to cook, make your salsa by mixing all salsa ingredients in a medium bowl.
6. Once halibut is cooked, remove from oven and make a tear on top. Be careful of the steam as it is very hot. Equally divide salsa and spoon ¼ of salsa on top of halibut through the slit you have created.

Curry Salmon with Mustard

Preparation Time: 10 minutes

Cooking Time: 8 minutes

Servings: 4

Ingredients:

- ¼ teaspoon ground red pepper or chili powder
- ¼ teaspoon ground turmeric

- ¼ teaspoon salt
- 1 teaspoon honey
- ½ minced clove garlic
- 2 teaspoons whole grain mustard
- 4 pcs 6-oz salmon fillets

Directions:

1. In a small bowl mix well salt, garlic powder, red pepper, turmeric, honey and mustard.
2. Preheat oven to broil and grease a baking dish with cooking spray.
3. Place salmon on baking dish with skin side down and spread evenly mustard mixture on top of salmon.
4. Pop in the oven and broil until flaky around 8 minutes. Serve.

Crisped Coco-Shrimp with Mango Dip

Preparation Time: 10 minutes

Cooking Time: 20 minutes

Servings: 4
Ingredients:
- 1 cup shredded coconut
- 1 lb. raw shrimp, peeled and deveined
- 2 egg whites
- 4 tablespoon tapioca starch
- Pepper and salt to taste

Directions:
1. Preheat oven to 400°F. Take a pan with a wire rack on top.
2. In a medium bowl, add tapioca starch and season with pepper and salt.
3. In a second medium bowl, add egg whites and whisk.
4. In a third medium bowl, add coconut.
5. To ready shrimps, dip first in tapioca starch, then egg whites, and then coconut. Place dredged shrimp on wire rack. Repeat until all shrimps are covered. Pop shrimps in the oven and roast for 10 minutes per side.
6. Meanwhile make the dip by adding all ingredients in a blender. Puree until smooth and creamy. Transfer to a dipping bowl. Once shrimps are golden brown, serve with mango dip.

MANGO DIP:
- 1 cup mango, chopped
- 1 jalapeño, thinly minced
- 1 teaspoon lime juice
- 1/3 cup coconut milk
- 3 teaspoon raw honey

Dill Relish on White Sea Bass

Preparation Time: 10 minutes
Cooking Time: 12 minutes
Servings: 4
Ingredients:
- 1 ½ tablespoon chopped white onion
- 1 ½ teaspoon chopped fresh dill
- 1 lemon, quartered
- 1 teaspoon Dijon mustard
- 1 teaspoon lemon juice
- 1 teaspoon pickled baby capers, drained
- 4 pieces of 4-oz white sea bass fillets

Directions:
1. Preheat oven to 375°F. Prepare four aluminum foil squares and place 1 fillet per foil.
2. Mix lemon juice, mustard, dill, capers and onions in a small bowl. Squeeze a lemon wedge per fish. Divide into 4 the dill spread and drizzle over fillet. Close the foil over the fish securely and pop in the oven. Bake for 12 minutes or until fish is cooked through. Remove from foil and transfer to a serving platter, serve and enjoy.

Dijon Mustard and Lime Marinated Shrimp

Preparation Time: 10 minutes
Cooking Time: 10 minutes
Servings: 8
Ingredients:
- ½ cup fresh lime juice, and lime zest as garnish
- ½ cup rice vinegar
- ½ teaspoon hot sauce
- 1 bay leaf
- 1 cup water
- 1 lb. uncooked shrimp, peeled and deveined
- 1 medium red onion, chopped
- 2 tablespoon capers
- 2 tablespoon Dijon mustard
- 3 garlic cloves

Directions:
1. Mix hot sauce, mustard, capers, lime juice and onion in a shallow baking dish and set aside.
2. Bring to a boil in a large saucepan bay leaf, cloves, vinegar and water. Once boiling, add shrimps and cook for 1 minute stirring continuously. Drain shrimps and pour shrimps into onion mixture.
3. For 1 hour, refrigerate while covered the shrimps.
4. Then serve shrimps cold and garnished with lime zest. Enjoy!

Conclusion

Thank you for reading this book!

I hope these recipes could help you to start having healthy habits eating delicious meals!

As I said at the beginning of this book, I created this book to allow busy people to eat healthy without renounce of taste!

Regardless of the diet people could follow, the key is to vary the foods and take the right amount of daily nutrients!

A weight maintenance's and prevent disease key is **"To have healthy habits"**: this includes a **healthy lifestyle**, a **equilibrate diet** and **fitness exercise regularly**.

I suggest you follow this easy 21-Meal Plan to start creating your healthy habits and do about 30 minutes of soft exercise every day.

It's a great way to start your health journey!

Thanks very much for reading, and I wish you to achieve all your goals!

Michelle Laurie Johnson

CPSIA information can be obtained
at www.ICGtesting.com
Printed in the USA
BVHW011349270421
605941BV00003B/292